INSTITUTE OF
GOVERNMENTAL
STUDIES

University of California, Berkeley

SENTENCING THE OFFENDER —

A Bibliography

Compiled by
Dorothy Campbell Tompkins

March 1971

INSTITUTE OF GOVERNMENTAL STUDIES

Eugene C. Lee, *Director*

The Institute of Governmental Studies was established in 1921 as the Bureau of Public Administration, and given its present name in 1962. One of the oldest organized research units in the University of California, the Institute conducts extensive and varied research and service programs in public policy, politics, urban-metropolitan problems, and public administration.

A prime resource in these endeavors is the Institute's public affairs library, comprising over a quarter of a million documents, pamphlets, and periodicals related to government and public affairs. The library serves faculty and staff members, students, public officials, and interested citizens.

The Institute's professional staff is composed of faculty members who hold joint Institute and departmental appointments, research specialists, librarians, and graduate students from a variety of social science disciplines. In addition, the Institute is host to visiting scholars from other parts of the United States and many foreign nations.

The Institute publishes books, monographs, periodicals, reprints, reports, and bibliographies for a nationwide readership. The publications are intended to stimulate research, thought, and action by scholars and public officials, with respect to significant governmental and social issues.

Sentencing the Offender

INSTITUTE OF
GOVERNMENTAL
STUDIES
University of California, Berkeley

SENTENCING THE OFFENDER—
A Bibliography

Compiled by
Dorothy Campbell Tompkins

March 1971

International Standard Book Number (ISBN) 0-87772-080-0
Library of Congress Catalog Card Number: 75-634804
$3.50

PREFACE

The preparation of this bibliography was prompted by news reports of "longer than life" sentences (500 years, 1000 years) in Oklahoma and Texas during September and October 1970. It is concerned with materials on court sentencing of the offender published since 1956. It supplements, in part, my *Administration of Criminal Justice, 1949-1956, a Selected Bibliography*, published by the California State Board of Corrections and reprinted in 1970 by Patterson Smith Publishing Corporation.

In compiling this bibliography, use has been made of the Libraries of the University of California, Berkeley, particularly the Graduate Social Science, Law School, and Institute of Governmental Studies Libraries.

To the librarians on the Berkeley campus, who have assisted me in obtaining materials, and particularly my colleagues in the Institute of Governmental Stuies, I make grateful acknowledgment. To Judy Rasmussen, for her part in preparing the manuscript for publication and to John Barr Tompkins for his reading of the manuscript, I express my gratitude.

Dorothy Campbell Tompkins

March 1971

856333

CONTENTS

SENTENCING THE OFFENDER

"There is no decision in the criminal process that is as com-
plicated and difficult as the one made by the sentencing judge.
A sentence prescribes punishment, but it also should be the
foundation of an attempt to rehabilitate the offender, to in-
sure that he does not endanger the community, and to deter
others from similar crimes in the future. Often these objectives
are mutually inconsistent, and the sentencing judge must choose
one at the expense of the others."

> U. S. President's Commission on Law Enforcement and
> Administration of Justice
> The challenge of crime in a free society; a re-
> port. 340p Washington, D.C., February 1967
> C. 5: The courts (sentencing policies
> and procedures).
> Comment under title: The President's crime report
> and sentencing, by George H. Revelle. Trial
> Judges' Journal 6: 8+, July 1967.

"Law enforcement, judicial administration, and corrections are
inseparable parts of a seamless whole. The sentence is the end
product of the judicial part of the process, and it is remark-
able that so much attention has been given, for example, to
subtle niceties in regard to the admission of evidence, while
sentencing decisions...have all too often been left to hunch or
chance."

> Sentencing--a neglected issue; editorial. Judica-
> ture 53: 51, August-September 1969

Materials relating to the sentencing issue include the fol-
lowing--

Agata, Burton C.
　Time served under a reversed sentence or conviction--a pro-
　posal and a basis for decision. Montana Law Review 25: 1-
　74, Fall 1963
　　　　Appendix I: Statutes dealing with credit
　　　　for time served on reversed convictions
　　　　and sentences.

Alexander, Myrl E.
　A hopeful view of the sentencing process. American Crimi-
　nal Law Quarterly 3: 189-97, Summer 1965

American Bar Association. Section of Criminal Law
    Proceedings, August 6-8, 1962. 166p Chicago, 1963?
        Modern trends in sentencing, by George H.
        Boldt and others, p. 45-81.

American Bar Foundation
    Sentencing; the decision as to type, length, and conditions
    of sentence; by Robert O. Dawson. 428p (Administration of
    criminal justice series) Boston, Little Brown, 1969
            Pt. 1: Presentence information;
                 2: Probation system;
                 3: Determining the length of incar-
                    ceration;
                 4: The correctional process and the
                    legal system.

American Law Institute and American Bar Association. Joint
    Committee on Continuing Legal Education
    The problem of sentencing; by Sanford Kadish. 123p (Prob-
    lems in criminal law and its administration no. 10) Phila-
    delphia, 1962

American Society for Legal History
    Essays in jurisprudence in honor of Roscoe Pound; edited by
    Ralph A. Newman. 670p Indianapolis, Bobbs-Merrill, 1962
            Toward improved sentencing, by Sheldon
            Glueck, p. 410-38.

Barrett, Donald W.
    Sentence prediction and penalties: a sociological approach.
    Notre Dame Lawyer 35: 305-27, May 1960

Bazak, Yaakov
    Retribution as a consideration of sentencing policy. Delin-
    quency and Society (Jerusalem) 4 (1): 26-32, 1969
    Abstract: Crime and Delinquency Literature 2: 294, June
    1970.

Bennett, James V.
    Correctional problems the courts can help solve; before
    National Council on Crime and Delinquency, Advisory Coun-
    cil of Judges annual meeting, Boulder, June 26, 1960.
    Crime and Delinquency 7: 1-8, January 1961
            Includes: Sentencing procedures.

    Count-down for judicial sentencing; before Sixth Circuit
    Judiciary Conference, Dearborn, April 28, 1961. Bar Asso-
    ciation of District of Columbia, Journal 28: 420-29, August
    1961
    Same: Congressional Record, May 15, 1961: A3409-11; Federal
    Probation 25: 22-26, September 1961.

Bennett, James V.
    Memories of Sir Lionel Fox. Prison Service Journal (Great
    Britain) 111: 2-9, January 1964
            Concerning indeterminate sentencing and
            institutes in the United States.

    The sentence and treatment of offenders. Annals of Ameri-
    can Academy of Political and Social Science 339: 142-56,
    January 1962
            Includes: Federal sentencing procedure
            and California correctional system; Model
            Penal Code.

    The sentence--its relation to crime and rehabilitation. Law
    Forum (University of Illinois) (4): 500-11, Winter 1960

Blandin, Amos N., Jr.
    Fewer faces to haunt our dreams. Federal Probation 21: 9-
    14, December 1957
            Concerning design for sentencing--punish-
            ment is to reform.

Boldt, George H.
    Recent trends in criminal sentencing. American Correction-
    al Association, Annual Congress of Correction, Proceedings
    93: 32-37, 1963
    Same: Federal Probation 27: 3-6, March 1963.
            Concerning changing concept of punishment;
            disproportionate sentences; presentence
            reports; study prior to sentence; indeter-
            minate sentence.

Browdy, Joseph E. and Saltzman, Robert J.
    The effectiveness of the Eighth Amendment: an appraisal of
    cruel and unusual punishment. New York University Law Re-
    view 36: 846-75, April 1961

Campbell, William J. and Younger, Evelle J.
    Should sentencing be taken out of judges' hands? Federal
    Probation 26: 85, June 1962

Celler, Emanuel
    Society's stake in sentencing; before Judicial Conference
    of the Second Circuit, May 7, 1960. Brooklyn Barrister
    12: 49-54, November 1960

Chaffee, Bob
    Sentence aftermath. Presidio (Iowa State Penitentiary) 32
    (7): 20+, 1965
    Abstract: International Bibliography on Crime and Delin-

quency 3: 34, December 1965.
> Concerning tribunal plan in California and
> appellate review of criminal sentences in
> Massachusetts and Connecticut.

Chamber of Commerce of the United States
Marshaling citizen power against crime. 133p Washington, D.C., 1970
Excerpt: Congressional Record, February 2, 1971: H353-56.
> Includes: Sentences and dismissal or
> reduction of charges.

Clark, Tom C.
Sentencing and corrections. University of San Francisco Law Review 5: 1-9, October 1970

Cohen, Fred
...Evaluates M'Naghten rule, sentencing practice; before [Texas] Senate Committee for the Study of the Sociopathic Personality, April 11, 1964. Long Beach Bar Bulletin 10: 17-19, December 1964

Sentencing, probation and the rehabilitative ideal: the view from Mempa v. Rhay. Texas Law Review 47: 1-59, December 1968
> Concerning peno-correctional processes,
> especially sentencing and probation.

Conference of Chief Justices
Proceedings, twelfth annual meeting, August 23-28, 1960. 55p+ (mim) Chicago, Council of State Governments, 1961
> Includes: Judicial review of sentences
> in criminal cases.

Cooper, H. H. A.
A sentencing problem: how far is a fall from grace. Cleveland-Marshall Law Review 15: 587-97, September 1966
> Concerning three possible bases underly-
> ing sentences imposed by the courts--
> retribution, deterrence and reformation.

Craven, James C.
Sentencing. Law Forum (University of Illinois) 1966: 523-39, Fall 1966

Cross, Rupert
Sentencing in a rational society. Criminal Law Review 1970: 4-15, January 1970

De Ment, Ira
A plea for the condemned. Alabama Lawyer 29: 440-52, Oc-

tober 1968
>   Concerning a life sentence.

D'Esposito, Julian C., Jr.
>   Sentencing disparity: causes and cures. Journal of Criminal
>   Law... 60: 182-94, June 1969

Edwards, George
>   Society's stake in the criminal sentence. Texas Bar Journal
>   22: 426-31, August 22, 1959

>   Verdict: guilty--now what? NPPA News (National Probation
>   and Parole Association) 39: 1-4, March 1960

Elliott, E. L.
>   The enigma of sentencing--the individuality of man. Muni-
>   cipal Court Review 6: 27-29, April 1966

Excessive sentences; editorial. American Judicature Society,
>   Journal 41: 100-01, December 1957

Federal Bar Association of New York, New Jersey and Connecti-
>   cut. Committee on Criminal Law
>   The need for new approaches to sentencing. Criminal Law Bul-
>   letin 3: 682-85, December 1967

Flood, Gerald F.
>   Time and punishment--the judge's view. Prison Journal (Penn-
>   sylvania Prison Society) 41: 37-45, Autumn 1961

Frankel, Sandor
>   The sentencing morass, and a suggestion for reform. Crimin-
>   al Law Bulletin 3: 365-83, July-August 1967

Fricke, Charles W.
>   Sentence and probation; the imposition of penalties upon
>   convicted criminals. 96p Los Angeles, Legal Book Store,
>   1960

Friedman, Leonard M.
>   The dilemmas of sentencing. California State Bar Journal
>   44: 372-79, May-June 1969

Friends Committee on Legislation, San Francisco
>   Crime, the criminal law and criminal correction: a case for
>   reform; by Nathan Douthit. 58p 1966
>   Abstract: Crime and Delinquency Abstracts 5(2): 32, 1967.
>   >   Includes: Disparity in sentencing.

George, B. J., Jr.
>   Aggravating circumstances in American substantive and pro-

cedural criminal law; paper for the International Congress
of the International Association of Penal Law, 1964. University of Missouri at Kansas City Law Review 32: 14-32,
Winter 1964
> Concerning effect of aggravating factors
> on sentence for offenses against the per-
> son and against property.

Comparative sentencing techniques; before 19th annual conference of the federal judges of the Sixth Judicial Circuit,
Ann Arbor, June 5, 1958. Federal Probation 23: 27-31, March
1959

An unsolved problem; comparative sentencing techniques [in
other countries]. American Bar Association, Journal 45:
250-54, March 1959

Gernert, Paul J.
  The effects of length of sentencing upon parole. American
  Correctional Association, Annual Congress of Correction,
  Proceedings 93: 49-50, 1963

Gibbs, Jack P.
  Crime, punishment, and deterrence. Southwestern Social
  Science Quarterly 48: 515-30, March 1968
> Concerning relationship between criminal-
> homicide rates and estimates of the certain-
> ty and severity of imprisonment by states.

Granucci, Anthony F.
  "Nor cruel and unusual punishment inflicted"; the original
  meaning. California Law Review 57: 839-65, October 1969

Grygier, Tadeusz
  A computer-made device for sentencing decisions--is further
  counting and thinking really necessary? Journal of Research
  in Crime and Delinquency 6: 199-209, January 1969
> Concerning a device for predicting success
> on probation developed in a study of 973
> male probationers in Ontario.

Grygier, Tadeusz and Others, ed.
  Criminology in transition; essays in honour of Hermann Mannheim. 308p London, Tavistock Publications, 1965
> Sentencing in transition, by J. E. Hall
> Williams;
> Inquiry before sentence, by F. V. Jarvis.

Hebrew University of Jerusalem
  The causation and prevention of crime in developing countries; proceedings of the 12th International Course in

Criminology, September 2-20, 1962. 2v (Publication no. 5)
Jerusalem, October 1963
        Toward improved sentencing, by Sheldon
        Glueck, v. 2, p. 396-400.

Hill, Martin D.
    Modification of original sentence is a final, appealable
    order requiring the presence of the defendant. Law Forum
    (University of Illinois) 1964: 460-64, Summer 1964

Holt, Ivan Lee, Jr.
    The judge's attitude and manner at sentencing; before
    National Association of Municipal Judges, November 1962.
    Crime and Delinquency 10: 231-34, July 1964
    Condensed: Trial Judges' Journal 6: 7+, July 1967.

Hutton, Hampton
    Sentencing protection for the defendant. University of
    West Los Angeles Law Review 1: 59-66, June 1969

Inbau, Fred E.
    Public safety v. individual liberties; before National Dis-
    trict Attorneys' Association, Portland, July 26, 1961.
    Police Chief 29: 29-33, January 1962
            Concerning "turn em' loose" court
            decisions.

Individualized criminal justice in the Supreme Court: a study
    of dispositional decision making. Harvard Law Review 81:
    1260-79, April 1968

Is death for rape an excessive penalty? U.S. News and World
    Report, November 4, 1963: 10-11
            Three justices of the U.S. Supreme Court
            suggest it may be unconstitutional for a
            state to impose the death penalty on a
            rapist who has not endangered the life of
            his victim.

James, Howard
    Crisis in the courts. 267p New York, David McKay, 1968
        C. 10: The sentencing wonderland.
        Based on series of articles in Christian
        Science Monitor, April-July 1967.

Kadish, Sanford H.
    Legal norms and discretion in the police and sentencing
    processes. Harvard Law Review 75: 904-31, March 1962

Kaufman, Irving R.
    Sentencing: the judge's problem. Atlantic Monthly 205:

40-46, January 1960
Reprinted: Federal Probation 24: 3-10, March 1960.

Lane, Robert G.
Use of juvenile court records in fixing sentence in a sub-
sequent adult criminal proceeding. Southern California Law
Review 32: 207-11, Winter 1959
> Concerning a Pennsylvania case (Common-
> wealth v. Myers) allowing adult criminal
> sentence with past juvenile records in
> evidence and the access to juvenile rec-
> ords in California.

Levin, Gerald S.
Sentencing and guilty defendants. In Third criminal law
seminar, edited by Nathan Cohn, p. 158-72. Brooklyn, N. Y.,
Central Book Co., 1963

MacLeod, A. J.
If a penologist could become the sentencing judge; before
National Association of Municipal Judges, October 7, 1965.
Municipal Court Review 6: 22-25, April 1966

Mannheim, Hermann
Some aspects of judicial sentencing policy; before Univer-
sity of Pennsylvania Law School and others, May 1957. Yale
Law Journal 67: 961-81, May 1958
> Sentencing in its narrowest sense is the
> manner in which the courts when sentencing
> an offender use the discretion left to
> them by the law.

Moore, Bruce P.
Prisoners are people. Natural Resources Journal (University
of New Mexico School of Law) 10: 869-87, October 1970
> Includes: Sentencing techniques (senten-
> cing policy looking to cause and making
> it a personal process).

Morris, Norval
Prison in evolution. Federal Probation 29: 20-32, December
1965
> Includes: Sentencing practice.

Multiple offender--the effect of a suspended sentence in determining prior convictions. Albany Law Review 21: 125-31,
January 1957
> Concerning People v. Shaw, 150 N.Y.S. 2d 161.

Nagel, Stuart S.
Inequalities in the administration of criminal justice.

Trial Judges' Journal 5: 15+, April 1966
    "The disparities involving indigent de-
    fendants at the sentencing stage are sub-
    stantial."

The tipped scales of American justice: all citizens are
equal in court, but some are less equal than others. Transaction 3: 3-9, May-June 1966
    Includes: Conviction and sentencing.
    Based on American Bar Foundation data from
    state trial dockets (11,248 cases), in 1962.

Joint Commission on Correctional Manpower and Training
    The legal challenge to corrections: implications for man-
    power and training; a consultant's paper by Fred Cohen.
    107p Washington, D.C., March 1969
        C. 2: Sentencing (structure, disparity,
        plea bargaining, presentence reports,
        appellate review).

National Conference of State Trial Judges
    The trial judge and sentencing; by William K. Thomas and
    others. In its Eighth annual meeting, August 6-8, 1965,
    p. 4-32.
        Concerning problems of disparity, pre-
        sentence reports, mental defectives, pro-
        bation v. jail.

National Council on Crime and Delinquency. Council of Judges
    Proceedings, thirteenth annual meeting, Milwaukee, May
    1965. 78p New York, 1965
        Criminal Courts Section concerned with
        sentencing process.

National Council on Crime and Delinquency. National Parole
    Institutes
    The sentencing and parole process; by Daniel Glaser and Fred
    Cohen. 36p (mim) (Publication no. 4) New York, May 1964
    Same: 26p (JD-5001, Parole series) Washington, D.C., U.S.
    Office of Juvenile Delinquency and Youth Development, 1966.

Olmstead, Allen S., II
    "Suppose we change the subject." Federal Probation 28: 10-
    12, September 1964
        Why must an offender spend some time in
        jail? Do all offenders need punishment?

Packer, Herbert L.
    Making the punishment fit the crime. Harvard Law Review

77: 1071-82, April 1964
        Concerning Robinson v. California, 370 ·
        U.S. 660 (1962).

Palmore, John S.
    Sentencing and correction--the black sheep of criminal law.
    Federal Probation 26: 6-15, December 1962
    Same title: Review of Government (University of Kentucky,
    Bureau of Government Research) 3 (6), February 1963.

    Sentencing in criminal cases.   Kentucky State Bar Journal
    27: 5-8, July 1963

Parsons, James B.
    The personal factor in sentencing.   DePaul Law Review 13:
    1-14, Autumn 1963
        Concerning the rise of judicial discretion.

Paulsen, Monrad G. and Kadish, Sanford H., eds.
    Criminal law and its processes.   1189p   Boston, Little,
    Brown, 1962
        The sentencing process in a multiple goal
        system, p. 124-207.

Platz, William A.
    Criminal procedure changes; and, Sentencing, probation and
    parole; for 1962 Wisconsin Lawyers' Seminars.   42p   Madison,
    University of Wisconsin, Extension Law Department, 1962

Portman, Sheldon
    The defense lawyer's new role in the sentencing process.
    Federal Probation 34: 3-7, March 1970

Procedural due process at judicial sentencing for felony. Har-
    vard Law Review 81: 821-46, February 1968
        Concerning implications for sentencing
        procedure of various conceptions of sen-
        tencing and of recent Supreme Court treat-
        ment of the due process clause.

Rector, Milton G.
    Psychiatry as an aid to sentencing and probation; before
    National Association of Municipal Judges, Training Insti-
    tute, November 1964.   Municipal Court Review 5: 57-60,
    April 1965

Redmount, Robert S.
    Some basic considerations regarding penal policy.   Journal
    of Criminal Law... 49: 426-43, January-February 1959
        Includes: Sentencing practices.

Remington, Frank J. and Joseph, Allan J.
  Charging, convicting, and sentencing the multiple criminal
  offender. Wisconsin Law Review (4): 528-65, July 1961

Rice, Eugene
  Modern sentencing procedure; before Judicial Conference of
  the Tenth Circuit, Santa Fe, July 2-3, 1959. Oklahoma Law
  Review 13: 1-10, February 1960

Right to credit for time served and to preservation of the
  original sentence. Law Forum (University of Illinois) (1):
  180-92, Spring 1967

Robinson, Richard E.
  The defendant needs to know [about the sentence]. Federal
  Probation 26: 3-6, December 1962

The role of counsel at sentencing; symposium. Legal Aid Brief
  Case 23: 190-226, April 1965
              A defender's view, by Edwin L. Douglas;
              A prosecutor's view, by E. Lloyd Meeds;
              Appealing sentences in Massachusetts, by
              G. Joseph Tauro;
              Advocacy fully achieved, by Herbert J.
              Steffes;
              Requisites for sentencing, by Ivan Lee
              Holt, Jr.;
              Frivolous appeals, by Delmar Karlen;
              The appellate defender in Oregon, by Law-
              rence A. Aschenbrenner;
              Legal services to the indigent imprisoned,
              by Allan C. Hubanks and Llewellyn H.
              Linde;
              Due process in probation and parole rev-
              ocation proceedings, by Sol Rubin.

Rubin, Sol
  Allocation of authority in sentencing--correction decision;
  before second annual criminal law institute, University of
  Texas School of Law, September 8-10, 1966. Texas Law Review 45: 455-69, February 1967
              Concerning sentencing by jury, control of
              maximum term, minimum term, sentencing
              choices, controls of the sentencing choice.

  Disparity and equality of sentences--a constitutional challenge; before Colorado Judicial Conference, Colorado Springs,
  October 13, 1965. Federal Rules Decisions 40: 55-78, 1966

Rubin, Sol
  Illusions of treatment in sentences and civil commitments;
  before University of South Carolina, March 29, 1968. Crime
  and Delinquency 10: 79-92, January 1970
        Concerning drug cases.

  The law schools and the law of sentencing and correctional
  treatment. Texas Law Review 43: 332-43, February 1965

  Sentencing problems and solutions; before Association of
  Probation Officers for the Province of Ontario, Vineland,
  September 24, 1960. Canadian Journal of Corrections 4: 74-
  82, April 1962

Rubin, Sol and Others
  The law of criminal correction. 728p St. Paul, West Publishing Company, 1963
        Includes: The guilty plea and related
        sentence considerations; the presentence
        investigation and the hearing on the sen-
        tence; imposing sentence (by judge or jury);
        suspended sentence.

Saeed, Sultana
  Suspended sentences. Current Legal Problems 23: 71-97,
  1970

Scott, Bonnie B.
  Discriminatory sentencing and the unitary trial: two areas
  for application of the United States v. Jackson [390 U.S.
  570 (1968)] rationale. University of Pittsburgh Law Review
  31: 118-27, Fall 1969

Sentencing. NPPA Journal (National Probation and Parole Association) 2 (4), October 1956
        A judge's guide to sentencing, by Robert
        M. Hill;
        The purpose of the sentence, by Ira W.
        Jayne;
        The presentence investigation, by Ed-
        mond FitzGerald;
        Long prison terms and the form of sen-
        tence, by Sol Rubin;
        Sentencing and corrections, by Milton G.
        Rector;
        Sentencing the misdemeanant, by Thomas
        Herlihy, Jr.;
        Jury sentencing, by Charles O. Betts;
        The fine, by Charles H. Miller;
        Variations in sentencing, by George W.
        Davis.

Sentencing: a symposium. Law and Contemporary Problems 23:
399-582, Summer 1958
The aims of the criminal law, by Henry M.
Hart, Jr.;
Diagnostic techniques in aid of sentenc-
ing, by Ralph Brancale;
Predictive devices and the individualiza-
tion of justice, by Sheldon Glueck;
Sentencing by an administrative board, by
Norman S. Hayner;
Sentencing structure: its effect upon sys-
tems for the administration of justice, by
Lloyd E. Ohlin and Frank J. Remington;
Sentencing under the Model Penal Code, by
Paul W. Tappan;
A critique of the Model Penal Code sentenc-
ing proposals, by Will C. Turnbladh;
Comparative sentencing practice, by Her-
mann Mannheim.

Sentencing. Judicature (American Judicature Society) 53 (2),
August-September 1969
Sentencing--the need for alternatives, by
Paul W. Keve;
Sentencing reform and litigation, by Mil-
ton G. Rector;
Doubts about the indeterminate sentence,
by Bernard C. Kirby;
Ensuring rational sentences--the case for
appellate review, by Joseph D. Tydings;
Sentencing practices, problems and rem-
edies, by Walter S. Carr.

Sentencing selective service violators: a judicial wheel of
fortune. Columbia Journal of Law and Social Problems 5:
164-96, August 1969
Based on questionnaires received from
sixty-eight United States district judges.

Sigler, M. H.
How does length of prison sentence affect the management
and treatment of the offender? American Correctional Association, Annual Congress of Correction, Proceedings 93: 43-
48, 1963

Smith, William F.
Sentencing alternatives available to the courts. Federal
Probation 26: 3-5, June 1962
Includes: Prison or probation and indeter-
minate sentence.

Somit, Albert and Others
  Aspects of judicial sentencing behavior. University of
  Pittsburgh Law Review 21: 613-21, June 1960
        Concerning study of over two million cases
        decided in New York City Magistrates'
        Court, 1915-1930.

Statutory structures for sentencing felons to prison. Columbia Law Review 60: 1134-72, December 1960
        Includes table: General statutory pro-
        visions for sentencing felons, state-
        by-state.

Tappan, Paul W.
  Crime, justice and correction. 781p New York, McGraw-Hill,
  1960
        C. 15: Sanctions and sentencing.

The tasks of penology: a symposium on prisons and correctional
  law. Nebraska Law Review 45 (3), May 1966
        Toward a more enlightened sentencing pro-
        cedure, by Theodore Levin;
        Development and accomplishments of sen-
        tencing institutes in the federal judi-
        cial system, by L. W. Youngdahl.
  Same: edited by Harvey S. Perlman and Thomas B. Allington.
  241p Lincoln, University of Nebraska Press, 1969.

Thomas, D. A.
  Establishing a factual basis for sentencing. Criminal Law
  Review 1970: 80-90, February 1970

  Principles of sentencing. 350p (Cambridge studies in criminology v. 27) London, Heineman, 1970

  Sentencing co-defendants--when is uniform treatment necessary? Criminal Law Review 1964: 22-32, January 1964

  Sentencing--the basic principles. Criminal Law Review 1967:
  455-65, 503-25, August-September 1967

  Sentencing--the case for reasoned decisions. Criminal Law
  Review 1963: 243-53, April 1963

  Sentencing the mentally disturbed offender. Criminal Law
  Review 1965: 685-99, December 1965

Truax, Lyle H.
  Structuring the sentence; before sixteenth annual convention
  of Washington State Magistrates Association, Seattle. Judicature 52: 65-70, August-September 1968

Turkington, Richard C.
Unconstitutionally excessive punishments: an examination of the Eighth Amendment and the Weems principle. Criminal Law Bulletin 3: 145-66, April 1967

United Prison Association of Massachusetts
What's new in sentencing? 32p (process) (Bulletin no. 7) Boston, October 1957
Bibliography, p. 26-32.

U.S. Congress. Senate. Committee on the Judiciary. Subcommittee on National Penitentiaries
Of prisons and justice; a selection of the writings of James V. Bennett. 400p (88:2, S.Doc. no. 70) Washington, D.C., April 16, 1964
The sentence--its relation to crime and rehabilitation;
Countdown for judicial sentencing;
Toward a sentencing philosophy;
The sentence and treatment of offenders.

U.S. President's Commission on Law Enforcement and Administration of Justice. Task Force on Administration of Justice
Task force report: the courts. 178p Washington, D.C., 1967
C. 2: Sentencing (statutory sentencing framework, information for sentencing, exercise of court sentencing authority).
Appendix A: Perspectives on plea bargaining, by Arnold Enker.

U.S. President's Commission on Law Enforcement and Administration of Justice. Task Force on Corrections
Task force report: corrections. 222p Washington, D.C., 1967
C. 2: The role of corrections in intake and disposition (presentence investigation and diagnosis, diversion prior to adjudication, disposition pending trial).

Vasoli, Robert H.
Growth and consequences of judicial discretion in sentencing. Notre Dame Lawyer 40: 404-16, June 1965

Winningham, Richard H.
The dilemma of the directed acquittal. Vanderbilt Law Review 15: 699-719, June 1962
Concerning a uniform state policy and prac-

tice recognizing directed acquittals where
evidence is legally insufficient to support
a conviction.

Wolfgang, Marvin E., ed.
  Crime and culture; essays in honor of Thorsten Sellin. 462p
  New York, Wiley, 1968
        Sentencing re-visited, by Hermann Mann-
        heim, p. 349-79.

Younger, Evelle J.
  Probation and sentence. Los Angeles Bar Bulletin 38: 334-
  36+, August 1963
        How a lawyer can provide post-verdict as-
        sistance to defendant and court.

BIBLIOGRAPHIES

Abstracts on criminology and penology, v. 10, 1970+ Deventer, The Netherlands, 1970-

American Judicature Society
Sentencing patterns and problems: an annotated bibliography; by Walter S. Carr. 53p (process) (Report no. 28) Chicago, July 1969

California. State Library. Law Library
Index to California legal periodicals and documents, five year cumulation (1964-1968). 346p (mim) Sacramento, 1969

Harvard University. Law School. Library
Annual legal bibliography, v. 2, 1962+ Cambridge, 1962-

Index to legal periodicals, v. 50, August 1956-July 1957+ American Association of Law Libraries, 1957-

International bibliography on crime and delinquency, v. 1, no. 1, January 1963-v. 3, no. 8, June 1966. Bethesda, Md., U.S. National Clearinghouse for Mental Health Information, 1963-66
Continued by:
Crime and delinquency abstracts, v. 4, no. 1, 1966-v. 6, 1969.

SENTENCING PROCEDURES

Presentence Reports

"No defendant convicted of a crime involving moral turpitude, or a crime the sentence for which may include commitment for one year or more, shall be sentenced or otherwise disposed of before a written report of investigation by a probation officer is presented to and considered by the court." This is a provision of the Model Sentencing Act (Art. II, Sec. 2).

"Individualization in punishment has emerged as a guiding consideration of modern criminal science. The sentencing decision is no longer legislative in nature.... The judiciary has been vested with broad discretion and sentencing has become the most difficult and usually the only function of the criminal bench. Presentence reports are essential to the proper use of this discretion."

> Katkin, Daniel
> Presentence reports; an analysis of uses, limitations and civil liberties issues. Minnesota Law Review 55: 15-31, November 1970

Materials relating to presentence reports include the following--

Bartoo, Chester H.
Setting forth the adult defendant's previous arrest history in the probation report. California Probation, Parole and Correctional Association, Journal 1: 16-22, Spring 1964

Some hidden factors behind a probation officer's recommendations. Crime and Delinquency 9: 276-81, July 1963

Bates, Jerome E. and Zawadzki, Edward S.
Criminal abortion; a study in medical sociology. 250p Springfield, Ill., C. C. Thomas, 1964
C. 11: Presentence investigation in abortion cases.
Excerpt under title: Presentence investigation in abortion cases. Crime and Delinquency 9: 306-12, July 1963

Boston University. Law-Medicine Institute. Training Center in Youth Development
Techniques of probation. 254p (mim) Boston, [1966]
The art of the presentence report, by Paul W. Keve, p. 70-86.

Bowman, Charles H.
    A new modern code of criminal law.   FBI Law Enforcement Bul-
    letin 33: 14-17+, January 1964
            Concerning sentencing power taken from
            jury and presentence hearings in all cases.

Brennan, William J., Jr.
    Judicial supervision of criminal law administration; before
    National Council on Crime and Delinquency Advisory Council
    of Judges, May 30, 1963.   Crime and Delinquency 9: 227-34,
    July 1963

California. Board of Corrections
    Probation study, final report.   200p   Sacramento, September
    1965
            Presentence diagnosis for California
            superior courts, p. 83-86.

California. Department of Corrections
    Presentence diagnosis for California superior courts.   Its
    Correctional Review, September-October 1965: 16-18

[California. Department of Corrections. California Medical
    Facility]
    The use of Department of Corrections reception center diag-
    nostic services by California superior courts under Section
    1203.03 P.C. from 1957 to January 1, 1963; by Lloyd Braith-
    waite and Winslow Rouse.   [18p]   (ditto)   Sacramento, n.d.

California. University, Berkeley. School of Criminology
    The San Francisco Project: research report.   14nos   April
    1965-September 1969
            2: Three hundred presentence report recom-
            mendations.   12p   June 1965
            4: Federal probationers and prisoners:
            statutory sentencing alternatives and
            demographic data.   74p   December 1965
            5: Presentence report recommendations
            and demographic data.   72p   February
            1966
            7: Decision-making and the probation of-
            ficer: the presentence report recommenda-
            tion.   19p   June 1966

Carter, Robert M.
    It is respectfully recommended... [by a probation officer
    in a presentence report].   Federal Probation 30: 38-42,
    June 1966

Carter, Robert M.
  The presentence report and the decision-making process.
  Journal of Research in Crime and Delinquency 4: 203-11,
  July 1967
      Based on data compiled for San Francisco
      Project.

Carter, Robert M. and Gitchoff, G. Thomas
  The presentence report: an alternative format. Criminologica
  7: 58-67, February 1970
      Concerning an alternative experimentally
      used in courts of San Francisco.

Carter, Robert M. and Wilkins, Leslie T.
  Some factors in sentencing policy. Journal of Criminal Law
  ... 58: 503-14, December 1967
      Concerning relationship of presentence
      report to court disposition.

Cohn, Yona
  Criteria for the probation officer's recommendations to the
  juvenile court judge. Crime and Delinquency 9: 262-75,
  July 1963
      Concerning examination of 175 presentence
      investigation reports in Bronx Children's
      Court, New York City, January-June 1952.

  The presentence investigation report in the court: a corre-
  lation between the reporting probation officer and the court
  disposition. Thesis (D.Soc.Wk.), Columbia University, 1969
  Abstract: Social Service Review 43: 332, September 1969;
  Abstracts on Criminology and Penology 10: 347, May-June
  1970.

Colorado. Supreme Court
  [Sixteen amendments to the rules of criminal procedure ap-
  proved in 1961.] State Government News (Council of State
  Governments) 6: 12, February 1963
      Amendments include suppression of presentence
      reports and probation reports.

Criminal law--presentence investigation--right of confronta-
  tion. North Carolina Law Review 41: 260-67, 1963
      Concerning State v. Pope, 257 N.C. 326 (1962).

Employment of social investigation reports in criminal and
  juvenile proceedings. Columbia Law Review 58: 702-27, May
  1958
      "Use of pre-adjudication report appears
      to be unwise; juvenile is not informed
      of rights by probation officer."

Georgetown University. Law Center
A preliminary survey of the federal probation system; by
A. Kenneth Pye and others.   59p   Washington, D.C., March 4,
1963
        C. 3: Presentence investigation and report.

Gernert, Paul J.
    Why presentence investigation?   Pennsylvania Chiefs of Police
    Association, Bulletin 12: 5+, Spring 1961
            Concerning study of twelve cases by Penn-
            sylvania Board of Parole.

Gillick, John E., Jr. and Scott, Robert E., Jr.
    The presentence report: an empirical study of its use in the
    federal criminal process.   Georgetown Law Journal 58: 451-
    86, February 1970

Hoffman, Julius J.
    The probation officer's task is not a small one.   Federal
    Probation 22: 3-6, June 1958

Holtzoff, Alexander
    The criminal law and the probation officer.   Federal Proba-
    tion 23: 3-8, December 1959
            Concerning the problem of sentence; pre-
            sentence investigation; disparity in
            sentences.

Keve, Paul W.
    The probation officer investigates; a guide to the presen-
    tence report.   178p   Minneapolis, University of Minnesota
    Press, 1960

    The professional character of the presentence report.   Fed-
    eral Probation 26: 51-56, June 1962

Krasnow, Erwin G.
    Social investigation reports in the juvenile court: their
    uses and abuses.   Crime and Delinquency 12: 151-64, April
    1966

Lawton, Frederick
    Psychiatry, criminology and the law; before British Academy
    of Forensic Sciences, sixth annual meeting, July 17-18, 1965.
    Medicine, Science and the Law 5: 132-39, July 1965
            Concerning criticism of judge's failure
            to apply in sentencing the results of
            criminological research and findings of
            psychiatric clinical experience.
    Abstract: International Bibliography on Crime and Delinquency
    3: 47, December 1965.

Lederle, Arthur F.
   The public and the courts. Michigan State Bar Journal 37:
   8-13, July 1958
   Comment: Presentence report most important part of criminal
   procedure. Federal Probation 23: 63, March 1959.

Lehrich, Richard S.
   The use and disclosure of presentence reports in the United
   States. Federal Rules Decisions 47: 225-52, 1970

Manson, John R.
   Studying the offender before the court. Federal Probation
   33: 17-21, June 1969

Minnesota. Department of Corrections
   Creative thinking in corrections; presented at the annual
   institute of the Minnesota Corrections Association, St.
   Paul, October 2-4, 1961. 30p (process) St. Paul, 1961
         The presentence report, by Paul W. Keve,
         p. 1-11.

New York City, N.Y. Office of Probation
   [Many serious misdemeanants lack presentence study.] NCCD
   News (National Council on Crime and Delinquency) 45: 6,
   March-April 1966

Oregon. Judicial Council
   Second annual report, 1957. 11p (mim) Salem, August 1957
         Includes: Presentence investigation reports.

Oregon. Legislative Assembly. Legislative Interim Committee
   on Criminal Law
   Report on criminal law, in accordance with S.J.Res. no. 24,
   1959. 61p Salem, January 1961
         Presentence investigations, term of sus-
         pension or probation, revocation of proba-
         tion, p. 9-13.

Pennsylvania Association on Probation, Parole and Correction
   1963 conference proceedings. In its Quarterly 20 (2), June
   1963
         Presentence report, p. 71-75.

   Annual conference, Wilkes-Barre, May 23-26, 1965. In its
   Quarterly 22 (2), Summer 1965
         Workshop 4: Advantage of a presentence or
         prehearing investigation in the criminal
         courts, p. 41-45.

Peterson, Robert W.
   District of Columbia limits trial court's discretion to deny

request for presentence study. Stanford Law Review 17: 754-
62, April 1965
          Concerning Leach v. United States, 334 F.2d 945
          (1964).

Rubin, Sol
     Probation and due process of law; before Probation Associa-
     tion of New Jersey, March 21, 1962. Crime and Delinquency
     11: 30-38, January 1965
          Includes: Presentence investigation.

Saltman, Elias B.
     Pre-pleading investigation procedure for adult offenders.
     Correction (New York State Department of Correction) 24:
     15-17, March-April 1959

Smith, Charles E.
     Observation and study of defendants prior to sentence. Fed-
     eral Probation 26: 6-10, June 1962
          Concerning observation procedures in federal
          courts.

Smith, Rosser M.
     A probation officer looks at disparities in sentence. Fed-
     eral Probation 26: 19-23, December 1962

Stump, Lawrence M.
     Court investigations and reports. Federal Probation 21: 9-
     17, June 1957

Treger, Harvey
     A meaningful inquiry into the life of an offender; stress-
     ing the significant in the presentence investigation.
     Crime and Delinquency 11: 249-55, July 1965

Turner, James E.
     Nature of the presentence investigation. Alabama Correc-
     tional Research 4: 24-27, April 1957

U.S. Administrative Office of the United States Courts. Divi-
     sion of Probation
     The presentence investigation report. 39p (Publication no.
     103) Washington, D.C., February 1965
          Revision of 1943 manual of same title and
          includes presentence report outline and
          format, developed by Committee of Judicial
          Conference created to assist in adminis-
          tration of federal probation system.

U.S. Administrative Office of the United States Courts. Federal Probation Training Center, Chicago
Presentence investigation practices in the federal courts; by Jacob B. Barnett and others. 28p (mim) Washington, D.C., 1957
Summary under same title: by David H. Gronewald. Federal Probation 22: 27-32, September 1958.

Use of the presentence investigation in Missouri [authorized by Laws of 1957]. Washington University Law Quarterly 1964: 396-410, June 1964

Vann, Carl R.
Pretrial determination and judicial decision-making; an analysis of the use of psychiatric information in the administration of criminal justice; before Midwest Conference of Political Scientists, April 30-May 2, 1964. University of Detroit Law Journal 43: 13-33, October 1965
> Study of court and hospital case records
> in New York, 1950-1960, indicated trend
> toward harsher sentences for persons
> sent for psychiatric examination and
> found capable of standing trial.

Washington. Department of Institutions. Division of Research
Program evaluation: one model and a program approach (presentence report) for probation and parole; by Robert M. Carter. 19p (Research report v. 2, no. 3) Olympia, April 1969

Variations in presentence report recommendations and court dispositions; by Robert M. Carter. p. 27-33 (Research report v. 2, no. 5) Olympia, November 1969
> Study of 455 presentence report cases,
> July 1, 1968-April 30, 1969.

Washington. State Legislative Council
Eighth biennial report...submitted to the 38th Legislature. 80p Olympia, January 1963
> Juvenile traffic offenders presentence
> reports, p. 36-40.

Confidentiality of Reports

Appeals Court considers right to see probation reports. Federal Probation 25: 80, March 1961
> Does the U.S. Court of Appeals have the
> power to compel a U.S. District Court to
> turn over to it confidential presentence
> reports prepared by the District Court's
> probation officer?

Bach, Maxim N.
  The defendant's right of access to presentence reports.
  Criminal Law Bulletin 4: 160-70, April 1968

Barnett, Jacob B. and Gronewold, David H.
  Confidentiality of the presentence report. Federal Probation 26: 26-30, March 1962

Criminal law--presentence investigation--defendant does not
  have right of access to confidential documents used in determining sentence. Arizona Law Review 5: 127-30, Fall
  1963
          Concerning Williams v. New York, 337 U.S.
          241 (1948).

Guzman, Rafael
  Defendant's access to presentence reports in federal criminal courts. Iowa Law review 52: 161-85, October 1966

Higgins, John P.
  Confidentiality of presentence reports. Albany Law Review
  28: 12-44, January 1964

Legg, Lorraine O.
  Federal rule of criminal procedure 32 (c) (2): confidentiality or constitutionality? Lincoln Law Review 2: 66-75, December 1966

Lorensen, Willard D.
  The disclosure to defense of presentence reports in West
  Virginia. West Virginia Law Review 69: 159-66, February
  1967

Ohio law [approved June 24, 1963] makes probation reports confidential. Federal Probation 27: 76, December 1963

Parsons, James B.
  The presentence investigation report must be preserved as a
  confidential document. Federal Probation 28: 3-7, March 1964

Roche, Albert W.
  The position for confidentiality of the presentence investi-
  gation report. Albany Law Review 29: 206-24, June 1965
  Comment: In response to Roche, by John P. Higgins. Albany
  Law Review 29: 225-30, June 1965.

Schaffer, Benson
  The defendant's right of access to presentence reports. Criminal Law Bulletin 3: 674-81, December 1967.

Stanislaus, John N.
  Probation in the Model Penal Code; a resume and critique; before 49th annual New York State Conference on Probation, October 29, 1957. Correction (New York State Department of
  Correction) 22: 13-15, November-December 1957
          Concerning confidentiality of presentence
          reports.

Thomsen, Roszel C.
  Confidentiality of the presentence report: a middle position; before Inservice Training Institute of Federal Probation System, Annapolis, October 10, 1962. Federal Probation
  28: 8-10, March 1964

Wilson, John J.
  A new arena is emerging to test the confidentiality of presentence reports. Federal Probation 25: 6-11, December
  1961
          Concerning Williams v. New York, 337 U.S.
          241 (1949), and Federal Rules of Criminal
          Procedure, Rule 32 (c) (1).

Plea Bargaining

Plea bargaining is a process of negotiation in which the prosecutor offers the defendant certain concessions in exchange for
a guilty plea.

      The unconstitutionality of plea bargaining. Har-
      vard Law Review 83: 1387-411, April 1970

Materials relating to plea bargaining include the following--

Alschuler, Albert W.
  The prosecutor's role in plea bargaining. University of
  Chicago Law Review 36: 50-112, 1968

American Bar Foundation
  Conviction: the determination of guilt or innocence without
  trial; by Donald J. Newman. 259p (Survey of the administration of criminal justice in the United States) Boston,
  Little, Brown, 1966
          Concerning accuracy and fairness of guilty
          plea convictions; conviction of the maxi-
          mum offense on a plea of guilty; the nego-
          tiated plea; charge reduction and acquittal
          of the guilty to control other parts of the
          criminal justice process.

Another look at unconstitutional conditions [including judicial bargaining]. University of Pennsylvania Law Review
117: 144-82, November 1968

Ariano, Frank V. and Countryman, John W.
The role of plea negotiation in modern criminal law. Chi-
cago-Kent Law Review 46: 116-22, Spring-Summer 1969

Bongiovanni, Joseph N., Jr.
Guilty plea negotiation. Duquesne Law Review 7: 542-48,
Summer 1969

Chalker, Susan M.
Judicial myopia--differential sentencing and the guilty plea
--a constitutional examination. American Criminal Law Quarterly 6: 187-99, Summer 1968

Constitutional law--plea bargaining--New Jersey statute allow-
ing a defendant to avoid the death penalty by pleading non
vult or nolo contendere held valid. New York University Law
Review 44: 612-22, May 1969
          Concerning State v. Farcella, 52 N.J. 263
          (1968).

Cressey, Donald R. and Ward, David A., eds.
Delinquency, crime and social process. 1151p New York, Har-
per and Row, 1969
          Pleading guilty for considerations: a
          study of bargain justice, by Donald J.
          Newman, p. 220-33.

Criminal law--constitutional law--plea of guilty induced by a
promise of leniency. Texas Law Review 36: 97-100, November
1957
          Concerning Shelton v. United States, 246
          F. 2d 571 (1957).

Criminal law--plea bargaining. West Virginia Law Review 71:
59-64, December 1968

Criminal law--plea of guilty--voluntariness of plea of guilty
made in response to promise of leniency. New York University Law Review 35: 284-89, January 1960
          Concerning Martin v. United States, 256
          F.2d 345 (1959).

Criminal law--"voluntary" as applied to a plea of guilty. Alabama Law Review 10: 186-92, Fall 1957

Criminal procedure--duty of the trial judge to advise a defendant of the consequences of a guilty plea. South Carolina Law
Review 19: 261-68, 1967
         Concerning Thompson v. State, 151 S.E. 2d
         221 (1966).

Criminal procedure--inquiry into guilty pleas--Rule 11 of the
Federal Rules of Criminal Procedure. South Carolina Law Review 18: 668-75, 1966
         Concerning United States v. Rizzo, 362 F.
         2d 97 (1966).

Downie, Leonard, Jr.
Crime in the courts: assembly line justice. Washington
Monthly 2: 26-39, May 1970

Eiseland, Gregory A.
The guilty plea in South Dakota. South Dakota Law Review
15: 66-79, Winter 1970
         Concerning State v. Brech, 169 N.W. 2d
         242 (1969).

Fay, E. Dwight
The "bargain for" guilty plea. Criminal Law Bulletin 4:
265-72, June 1968

Fletcher, Robert L.
Pretrial discovery in state criminal cases. Stanford Law
Review 12: 293-322, March 1960
         Discovery for him who pleads guilty--
         bargain justice, p. 316-19.

Folberg, H. Jay
The "bargained for" guilty plea--an evaluation. Criminal
Law Bulletin 4: 201-12, May 1968

Gentile, Carmen L.
Fair bargains and accurate pleas. Boston University Law Review 49: 514-51, 1969

Guilty pleas [McMann v. Richardson, 397 U.S. 759: Brady v.
United States, 397 U.S. 742; Parker v. North Carolina, 397
U.S. 790 (1970)]. Journal of Criminal Law... 61: 521-26,
December 1970

Hall, Livingston and Others
Modern criminal procedure, cases, comments and questions.
ed.3 1456p St. Paul, West Publishing Co., 1969
         Coerced, induced and negotiated guilty
         pleas, p. 924-1000.

Heath, Robert L.
  Plea bargaining--justice off the record [in Kansas]. Wash-
  burn Law Journal 9: 430-43, Spring 1970

The influence of the defendant's plea on judicial determination of sentence. Yale Law Journal 66: 204-22, December
  1956

Kuh, Richard H.
  Plea copping. New York County Lawyers' Association, Bar Bulletin 24 (4): 160-67, 1966/67

La Fave, Wayne R.
  Sentencing the guilty plea defendant. American Trial Lawyer
  3: 14-15, December-January 1966/67

McIntyre, Donald M. and Lippman, David
  Prosecutors and early disposition of felony cases. American
  Bar Association, Journal 56: 1154-59, December 1970
      Table: Major dispositional points in
      felony cases (including guilty pleas).

Moon, Travis W.
  Criminal procedure--requirements for acceptance of guilty
  pleas. North Carolina Law Review 48: 352-61, Fall 1970

Morris, Norval and Davis, Edward M.
  Are courts too soft on criminals? Probation and plea bargaining in metropolitan jurisdictions; before National Conference
  of Metropolitan Court Judges, eighth annual meeting, October
  15-17, 1969. Judicature (American Judicature Society) 53:
  231-36, January 1970

New York State. Legislature. Joint Legislative Committee on
  Crime, Its Causes, Control and Effect on Society
  Report. 2nos (Legislative document (1968 no. 81, (1969)
  no. 16) Albany, September 1968, December 15, 1969
      Includes: Guilty plea bargaining.

Official inducements to plead guilty: suggested morals for a
  marketplace. University of Chicago Law Review 32: 167-87,
  Autumn 1964

Owens, Claude
  Plea bargaining...agreeing...recommending? Legal Aid Brief
  Case 26: 55-61, December 1967
      American Bar Association Advisory Committee
      on Criminal Trial calls plea bargaining,
      plea discussing-plea agreeing.

Polstein, Robert
   How to "settle" a criminal case. Practical Lawyer 8: 35-44, January 1962

Rosett, Arthur
   The negotiated guilty plea. Annals of American Academy of Political and Social Science (374): 70-81, November 1967

Schwartz, Murray L.
   Cases and materials on professional responsibility and the administration of criminal justice. 204p San Francisco, Matthew Bender and Co., 1962

Stein, Stanley M.
   Criminal procedure--plea bargaining--the Supreme Court of Pennsylvania has held that any participation by a trial judge in the plea bargaining process prior to trial is forbidden. Duquesne Law Review 8: 461-70, Summer 1970
            Concerning Commonwealth v. Evans, 252
            A. 2d 689 (1969).

Steinberg, Harris B. and Paulsen, Monrad G.
   A conversation with defense counsel on problems of a criminal defense. Practical Lawyer 7: 25-43, May 1961

Thomas, Paul
   Plea bargaining and the Turner case. Criminal Law Review 1970: 559-66, October 1970

Thompson, William J.
   The judge's responsibility on a plea of guilty; before West Virginia Judicial Association, October 23, 1959. West Virginia Law Review 62: 213-22, April 1960

Underwood, Robert C.
   Let's put plea discussions--and agreements--on record. Loyola University of Chicago Law Journal 1: 1-14, Winter 1970

[United States] Supreme Court upholds plea bargaining. NCCD News (National Council on Crime and Delinquency) 50: 6, January-February 1971
            Concerning North Carolina v. Alford,
            November 23, 1970.

Vetri, Dominick R.
   Guilty plea bargaining: compromises by prosecutors to secure guilty pleas. University of Pennsylvania Law Review 112: 865-908, April 1964
            Concerning plea bargaining as practiced
            by 205 prosecutors in most populous counties of 43 states.

Whitman, Peter A.
    Judicial plea bargaining. Stanford Law Review 19: 1082-92,
    May 1967
            Concerning United States ex rel. Elksnis
            v. Gilligan, 256 F. Supp. 244 (1966).

Delay in Sentencing

"Statutory provisions have been enacted setting forth standards as to when sentence should be imposed after conviction.
Because most statutes only provide that sentencing must be
within a reasonable time after the plea or verdict, they have
not solved the question as to what is a timely sentence."

    Hurd, David N.
        The imposition of sentence within a timely
        period after conviction [in New York]. Syra-
        cuse Law Review 13: 464-72, Spring 1962

Materials relating to delay in sentencing include the follow-
ing--

Banfield, Laura and Anderson, C. David
    Continuances in the Cook County criminal courts. University
    of Chicago Law Review 35: 259-316, Winter 1968

Criminal law--indefinite postponement of·sentence. University
    of Florida Law Review 11: 375-77, Fall 1958
            Concerning Helton v. State, 106 S. 2d 79
            (1958).

Criminal law--sentence--unreasonable delays--failure to sen-
    tence causes court to lose jurisdiction. Albany Law Review
    26: 330-34, 1962
            Concerning People ex. rel. Harty v. Fay,
            179 N.E. 2d 483 (1961).

Criminal procedure--sentencing--unreasonable delay in imposing
    sentence caused trial court to lose jurisdiction subsequent-
    ly to impose sentence. St. John's Law Review 36: 337-51,
    May 1962
            Concerning People ex. rel. Harty v. Fay,
            179 N.E. 2d 483 (1961).

Immediate sentencing proposed for Pennsylvania [by Criminal
    Procedural Rules Committee]. Judicature (American Judica-
    ture Society) 53: 83, August-September 1969

Iowa. State University of Science and Technology. Department of
Economics and Sociology
Time lapse in criminal litigation in Iowa; by Walter A. Lun-
den. 39p Ames, 1964

A time study of criminal litigation in Boone and Story Coun-
ties, Iowa, 1955-1957; by Walter A. Lunden and David Schmei-
ser. 17p (ditto) Ames, December 18, 1961

Lunden, Walter A.
Time lapse between sentence and execution: the United States
and Canada compared. American Bar Association, Journal 48:
1043-45, November 1962

Addressing the Court

"The right of a prisoner to speak in his own behalf before sentencing was recognized by the common law as early as 1689....
Although allocution procedure has been carried forward into modern law, in the majority of the jurisdictions in the United
States...the trend...is to regard allocution as a mere formality
the omission of which is not reversible error."

> Criminal procedure--right of defendant to make
> statement before sentencing. Tulane Law Re-
> view 35: 831-33, June 1961
> > Concerning Green v. United States,
> > 365 U.S. 301 (1961).

Materials relating to allocution include the following---

Court should afford the defendant a personal opportunity to
speak before sentence is pronounced. American University
Law Review 6: 117-19, June 1957
> Concerning Couch v. United States,
> 235 F. 2d 519 (1956).

Criminal law--judgment and sentence--right to allocution. University of Kansas Law Review 11: 270-72, December 1962
> Concerning Kansas and United States
> Supreme Courts.

Federal post-conviction remedies cannot be employed to attack
failure to comply with sentencing procedure of criminal rule
32 (a). Columbia Law Review 61: 885, 1962
> Concerning Hill v. United States,
> 368 U.S. 424 (1962).

Sentencing by Jury

"In general under American law the jury does not deal with penalty.... In a fifth of the states, chiefly in the South, the
penalties for all cases are determined by the jury, within the
framework established by the legislature, and in three states
the jury sets the penalty only for certain specific offenses."

> Kalven, Harry, Jr. and Zeisel, Hans
> The American jury. 559p Boston, Little,
> Brown, 1966
> C. 20: Defendant has been punished
> enough, footnote 1.

Materials relating to jury sentencing include the following--

California Supreme Court upholds jury discretion to impose
death penalty. Journal of California Law Enforcement 3: 142-
50, January 1969
> Concerning cases of Anderson and Sater-
> field, November 18, 1966.

Glenn, Franklin P.
The California penalty trial. California Law Review 52: 386-
407, May 1964
> Includes: Jury discretion in sentencing
> in capital cases.

Jury sentencing in Virginia. Virginia Law Review 53: 968-1001,
May 1967
> Concerning question of whether the jury
> should be the sentencing authority in
> noncapital cases.

Knowlton, Robert E.
Problems of jury discretion in capital cases. University of
Pennsylvania Law Review 101: 1099-136, June 1953

LaFont, H. M.
Assessment of punishment--a judge or jury function [in Texas].
Texas Law Review 38: 835, October 1960

Morris, Leslie W., II
Criminal procedure--what agency should fix sentence? Kentucky Law Journal 46: 260-70, Winter 1958
> "Sentencing should be left to some perman-
> ent, experienced agency and not to the jury."

Stubbs, Robert S. II
Jury sentencing in Georgia--time for a change? Georgia State
Bar Journal 5: 421-30, May 1969

A study of the California penalty jury in first-degree murder
  cases. Stanford Law Review 21: 1297-497, June 1969
          Concerning a study of 238 cases,
          1958-66.

Togman, Leonard S.
  The two-trial system in capital cases. New York University
  Law Review 39 (1): 50-77, January 1964

U.S. Solicitor General
  [Urged the U.S. Supreme Court to leave to the state legis-
  latures and to Congress the decision of how capital punishment should be handled by trial juries, in relation to cases
  of Dennis C. McGautha and James E. Crampton.] NCCD News
  (National Council on Crime and Delinquency) 50: 7, January-
  February 1971

Webster, Charles W.
  Jury sentencing--grab bag justice. Southwestern Law Journal
  14: 221-30, Spring 1960
          Study of crimes of murder, rape and nar-
          cotics in District Court of Dallas County,
          1958-1959.

Williams, J. E. Hall
  Jury discretion in murder trials. Modern Law Review 17: 315-
  28, July 1954

Wolf, Edwin D.
  Abstract of analysis of jury sentencing in capital cases:
  New Jersey, 1937-1961. Rutgers Law Review 19: 56-64, Fall
  1964

Indeterminate Sentence

"When the time of release of a prisoner is determined by an administrative board and the court merely imposes minimum and maximum limits of the penalty, the sentence is known as indeterminate sentence. Technically, the sentence is not indeterminate
if the limits are fixed by the court or by the legislature, and
it should be called indefinite rather than indeterminate."

      Branham, Vernon C. and Kutash, Samuel B., eds.
        Encyclopedia of criminology. 527p New York,
        Philosophical Library, 1949

Materials relating to indeterminate sentence include the fol-
lowing--

Crain, William W.
  Indeterminate and determinate time in the treatment of the

adolescent delinquent. Federal Probation 26: 28-32, September 1962

Hayner, Norman S.
Setting the minimum sentence in Washington state. Journal of Criminal Law... 49: 335-37, November-December 1958

Illinois. Legislative Council
Some aspects of indeterminate sentence and parole laws. 35p (process) (Publication no. 130) Springfield, February 1957
   Appendix: Citations to indeterminate sentence provisions of state parole laws.

Indeterminate sentence--half step toward science in law. Western Reserve Law Review 10: 574-85, September 1959

Institute for the Study of Crime and Delinquency
Estimating prison and parole terms under an indeterminate sentence law: social effectiveness study, California Medical Facility, Vacaville, California; by Don M. Gottfredson and Kelley B. Ballard, Jr. 151p (Report no. 5) Sacramento, July 1964
   Concerning study of 2,154 men before parole board, May 1, 1962-April 30, 1963.

Estimating sentences under an indeterminate sentence law; by Don M. Gottfredson and Kelley B. Ballard, Jr. Sacramento, July 1965

Mitford, Jessica
Kind and usual punishment in California. Atlantic Monthly 227: 45-52, March 1971
   Includes: Indeterminate sentence.

Randolph, Ross V.
Are long sentences necessary? American Journal of Correction 21: 4-5+, March-April 1959
   Concerning consideration of indefinite sentences.

Reich, Miriam
Therapeutic implications of the indeterminate sentence. Issues in Criminology (University of California, Berkeley) 2: 7-28, Spring 1966

Schreiber, Aaron M.
Indeterminate therapeutic incarceration of dangerous criminals: perspectives and problems. Virginia Law Review 56: 602-34, May 1970

Smith, Kathleen J.
  A cure for crime: the case for the self-determinate prison
  sentence. 112p London, Duckworth, 1965

Use of the indeterminate sentence in crime prevention and rehabilitation. Duke Law Journal 7: 65-87, Spring 1958

Williams, J. E. Hall
  Alternatives to definite sentences. Law Quarterly Review
  80 (317): 41-62, January 1964
      Concerning development of indeterminate
      sentence in the United States.

California

California. Legislature. Assembly. Interim Committee on Criminal Procedure
  Indeterminate sentence law; a public hearing, July 19, 1960
  90p (mim) Sacramento, 1960

Colorado

Colorado. Legislative Council
  Criminal laws and indeterminate sentencing. 35p (process)
  (Research publication no. 113) Denver, November 1966
      Sentencing and institutional programs,
      p. 25-35.

Indefinite sentencing and the Colorado correctional system.
  40p+ (process) (Research publication no. 139) Denver,
  December 1968

Scott, Austin W., Jr.
  Comment on indeterminate sentencing of criminals. Rocky
  Mountain Law Review 33: 544-52, June 1961

Tinsley, Harry C.
  Indeterminate sentencing of criminals. Rocky Mountain Law
  Review 33: 536-43, June 1961

Oklahoma

Criminal law--Oklahoma's indeterminate sentencing act [became
  effective January 1, 1964]. Tulsa Law Journal 1: 48-53,
  January 1964

Pennsylvania

Pennsylvania. Department of Justice. Bureau of Correction
  A review of sentences to the Bureau of Correction; a pilot

study involving indefinite sentences. 20p (mim) (BCR-RS, B-15, IC) Camp Hill, October 10, 1957

Tennessee

Prince, Matthew S.
The indeterminate sentence law in Tennessee [Acts of 1913, c. 8]. Tennessee Law Review 25: 366-74, Spring 1958

West Virginia

Brown, Londo H.
West Virginia indeterminate sentence and parole laws. West Virginia Law Review 59: 143-79, February 1957
>Second part of report to Joint Committee on Government and Finance and Commission on Interstate Cooperation of the West Virginia Legislature.

Consecutive Sentences

"If the termination of one sentence serves only as the beginning of another, perhaps in another institution, no plan of treatment can be said to exist. So existing law favors concurrent rather than consecutive terms."

>National Council on Crime and Delinquency. Advisory Council of Judges
>Model Sentencing Act. 35p New York, 1963

Materials relating to consecutive sentences includes the following--

Consecutive sentences in single prosecutions: judicial multiplication of statutory penalties. Yale Law Journal 67: 916-31, April 1958
>Concerning Gore v. United States, 244 F.2d 763 (1957).

Criminal law--commencement date of subsequent consecutive sentence when prior conviction reversed. Boston University Law Review 38: 623-25, Fall 1958
>Concerning Brown v. Commissioner of Correction (Mass.), 140 N.E. 2d 461 (1957).

Criminal law--successive sentences for separate refusals to answer related questions after a general refusal held improper multiplication of offenses. DePaul Law Review 7: 260-65, Spring-Summer 1958
>Concerning Yates v. United States, 356 U.S. 363 (1958).

Johnson, Phillip E.
Multiple punishment and consecutive sentences: reflections on the Neal doctrine. California Law Review 58: 357-90, March 1970

Merker, Mordecai M.
Multiple punishment in the federal courts: consecutive sentences based on overlapping statutes covering a single criminal transaction. American Criminal Law Quarterly 4: 206-10, Summer 1966

Increased Sentences

Under current criminal practice, whenever a defendant seeks reversal of his conviction and a retrial, he subjects himself to the risk of an increased sentence.

> Phillips, C. Alton
> Increased sentence upon retrial. Washington and Lee Law Review 25: 60-69, Spring 1968
> > Concerning Patton v. North Carolina,
> > 381 F. 2d 634 (1967).

Materials relating to increased sentences include the following--

Ashman, Allan
Prisoner's dilemma: harsher punishment upon retrial. American Bar Association, Journal 55: 928-31, October 1969
> Concerning North Carolina v. Pearce,
> 395 U.S. 711 (1969).

Brandon, Barbara
In Van Alstyne's wake: North Carolina v. Pearce. University of Pittsburgh Law Review 31: 101-17, Fall 1969
> Concerning State v. Pearce, 266 North
> Carolina 234 (1966).

Criminal law--resentencing jury may impose a harsher sentence on retrial. Vanderbilt Law Review 23: 859-67, May 1970
> Concerning Pinkard v. Henderson, 6 Crim.L.
> Rptr. 2148 (Tenn.Crim.App. 1969).

Devine, Myles J.
Solution to an "incredible dilemma"--the original sentence as a ceiling. South Dakota Law Review 13: 130-45, Winter 1968

Habeas corpus: unconstitutional increase in sentence upon retrial and denial of credit for time served: "jaws of the same vice." Duke Law Journal (4): 1172-81, Autumn 1966

Honigsberg, Peter J.
  Limitations upon increasing a defendant's sentence following a successful appeal and reconviction. Criminal Law Bulletin 4: 329-42, July-August 1968

Increased sentence upheld following invalidation of a sentence
  imposed in defendant's absence. Utah Law Review 1966: 280-
  88, July 1966
            Concerning James v. United States, 348
            F. 2d 430 (1965).

McElroy, Pender R.
  Criminal law--sentencing--denial of credit for time served
  or longer sentence imposed at retrial. North Carolina Law
  Review 46: 407-18, February 1968

Van Alstyne, William W.
  In Gideon's wake: harsher penalties and the "successful" criminal appellant. Yale Law Review 74: 606-39, March 1965

Williford, John W.
  Sentencing in criminal cases--new dilemma for trial judge.
  Georgia State Bar Journal 6: 183-88, November 1969
            Concerning North Carolina v. Pearce,
            395 U.S. 711 (1969).

Sentencing and Probation

"Sentencing is in large part concerned with avoiding future
crimes by helping the defendant learn to live productively in
the community which he has offended against. Probation pro-
ceeds on the theory that the best way to pursue this goal is
to orient the criminal sanction toward the community setting
in those cases where it is compatible with the other objectives of sentencing."

        American Bar Association. Project on Standards for
          Criminal Justice
          Standards relating to probation; recommended by
          the Advisory Committee on Sentencing and Review.
          110p (tentative draft) New York, Institute of
          Judicial Administration, February 1970

Materials relating to probation include the following--

Best, Judah and Birzon, Paul I.
  Conditions of probation: an analysis. Georgetown Law Journal 51: 809-36, Summer 1963

Borrillo, Theodore A.
  Probation: a sensible but sensitive approach to delinquency.
  Villanova Law Review 6: 480-502, Summer 1961

Carter, Robert M. and Wilkins, Leslie T., eds.
  Probation and parole: selected readings. 694p New York,
  Wiley, 1970

Elliott, Philip
  Can judges guide criminals to lawful living? [How far can
  a sentencing judge go in the matter of probation?] Michigan
  State Bar Journal 38: 50-58, November 1959

Murrah, Alfred
  Prison or probation-- which and why? before National Probation
  and Parole Association, August 23, 1955. Journal of Criminal
  Law... 47: 451-56, November-December 1956

Rector, Milton G.
  The effects of sentencing upon probation. American Correctional Association, Annual Congress of Correction, Proceedings 93: 38-42, 1963
  Same title: American Journal of Correction 25: 20+, September-October 1963.

Sanson, Don R.
  Summary probation; before Los Angeles County Municipal Judges
  Association, December 1963. CPPCA Journal (California Proba-
  tion Parole and Correctional Association) 1: 1-17, Fall 1964

Smith, Rosser M.
  A probation officer looks at disparities in sentence. Federal
  Probation 26: 19-22, December 1962

Tompkins, Dorothy C.
  Probation since World War II: a bibliography. 311p Ber-
  keley, University of California, Institute of Governmental
  Studies, 1964

Yankwich, Leon R.
  Individualization of punishment in the federal courts. Fed-
  eral Rules Decisions 20: 385-93, 1957
  Same title: Federal Probation 21: 3-6, March 1957.

Sentencing and Race

"The claim that criminal courts in the United States practice
racial discrimination in sentencing is widely affirmed in the
American literature of criminology. The research evidence on
which the charge is grounded is somewhat equivocal in that some
studies show a general tendency on the part of the court to impose heavier penalties on Negroes in comparison with whites,
while others show that for most offenses Negroes receive lighter
sentences."

> Green, Edward
> Inter- and intra-racial crime relative to sen-
> tencing. Journal of Criminal Law... 55: 348-
> 58, September 1964

Materials relating to sentencing and race include the follow-
ing--

Bullock, Henry A.
Significance of the racial factor in the length of prison
sentences. Journal of Criminal Law... 52: 411-17, November-
December 1961
> Based on study of 3,644 inmates in Texas
> State Prison, Huntsville, 1958.

Forslund, Morris A.
Age, occupation and conviction rates of white and Negro males:
a case study; before Rocky Mountain Social Science Association, 10th annual meeting, May 3-4, 1968. Rocky Mountain
Social Science Journal 6: 141-46, April 1969
> Study during 1958-61 in Stamford, Conn.
> of all males 16 years and over, arrested
> and charged with any offense other than
> motor vehicle law violation.

NAACP Legal Defense and Educational Fund, Inc.
[Conferences, in Virginia, April 13-16, 1967; in California,
June 8-11, 1967; set of material.] New York, New York Uni-
versity School of Law, Project on Social Welfare Law, 1967
> Includes: Lectures on sentencing.

Partington, Donald H.
The incidence of the death penalty for rape in Virginia.
Washington and Lee Law Review 22: 43-75, Spring 1965

Southern Regional Council
Race makes the difference; an analysis of sentence disparity
among black and white offenders in southern prisons. 16p
(mim) Atlanta, March 1969
> Based on data collected in Summer 1967 by

> law students for SRC's Project on Crime
> and Corrections in seven prison systems.

Syracuse University
  [Double jeopardy: black and poor; by Franklin H. Williams
  before Conference on Crime, on Capital Punishment and the
  Discriminatory Practices Which Are Followed.]
  Reprinted: Congressional Record, February 6, 1969: E909-12.

REVIEW OF SENTENCE

"In principle, judicial review should be available for all sentences imposed in cases where provision is made for the review of the conviction.... While the number of jurisdictions...in which review of sentence is available is steadily growing, it appears that review of the merits of a sentence has actually been undertaken by an appellate court in only twenty-one states. The number in which review is realistically available in every serious cases is much lower, something on the order of fifteen."

American Bar Association. Project on Minimum
Standards for Criminal Justice
Standards relating to appellate review of sentences; recommended by the Advisory Committee on Sentencing and Review. 160p (tentative draft) New York, Institute of Judicial Administration, April 1967
Appendix A: Review statutes [of 13 states and military courts].

Materials relating to review of sentence include the following--

Alaska. Judicial Council
[Recommendations on sentence appeal, sent to Supreme Court and Legislature, based on Sitka Conference; statute embodying the recommendations approved by 1969 Legislature (sec. 5, c. 117 SLA 1969, effective January 1, 1970.]

Appellate review of primary sentencing decisions: a Connecticut case study. Yale Law Journal 69: 1453-78, July 1960

Appellate review of sentencing procedure. Yale Law Journal 74: 379-89, December 1964
Concerning Leach v. United States, 334 F. 2d 945 (1964).

Baude, Patrick L.
Grounds for relief under 28 U.S.C. 2255: a suggested standard. American Criminal Law Quarterly 5: 112-24, Spring 1967
Concerning expansion of federal review of sentencing beyond that of habeas corpus.

Brewster, Leo
Appellate review of sentences; before Judicial Conference of Ninth Circuit, Sun Valley, July 15, 1965. Federal Rules Decisions 40: 79-88, 1965

Cofer, Hume
Code of criminal procedure provisions for new trial, arrest
of judgment, judgment, sentence and appeal. Texas Bar Journal 29: 15-16+, January 1966

Connecticut. Judicial Department
Report of Executive Secretary, 1957-1958. 42p Hartford,
1958
Analysis of Act establishing procedure
for review of sentences imposed by the
superior court, p. 40.

Council of State Governments. Committee of State Officials on
Suggested State Legislation
Program of suggested state legislation, 1962. 155p Chicago,
November 1961
Includes: Bill on review of sentences in
criminal cases (based on legislation in
force in Connecticut (1957) and Massachu-
setts (1943).

Program of suggested state legislation, 1963. 287p Chicago,
1962
Includes: Review of sentences in criminal
cases.

Criminal law--judicial review--appellate modification of exces-
sive sentence. Iowa Law Review 46: 159-66, Fall 1960
Concerning Smith v. United States, 273
F. 2d 462 (1959).

Criminal law--sentence--what is the proper scope of appellate
review of sentencing? Harvard Law Review 75: 416-18, December 1961

Criminal procedure--appealability of a criminal sentence--sen-
tence modified on appeal. Rutgers Law Review 16: 186-91,
February 1961
Concerning State v. Johnson, 170 A. 2d
830 (1961).

Criminal procedure--scope of appellate review of sentences in
capital cases. University of Pennsylvania Law Review 108:
434-49, January 1960
Concerning Commonwealth v. Green, 151 A. 2d
241 (1959) and Commonwealth v. Cater, 152 A.
2d 259 (1959).

DeCosta, Frank A., Jr.
Disparity and inequality of criminal sentences: constitutional and legislative approaches to appellate review and reallo-

cation of the sentencing function. Howard Law Journal 14:
29-59, Winter 1968

Dix, George E.
Judicial review of sentences: implications for individualized
disposition. Law and the Social Order (3): 369-418, 1969

Erwin, Martin N.
Appellate review of legal but excessive sentences. North
Carolina Law Review 44: 1118-26, June 1966

George, B. James, Jr.
Review of sentencing procedure is suggested; before Sixth
Circuit Judicial Conference. American Judicature Society,
Journal 42: 65, August 1958

Halperin, David J.
Appellate review of sentence in Illinois--reality or illu-
sion? Illinois Bar Journal 55: 300-14, December 1966
Illinois Code of Criminal Procedure granted
power to Appellate and Supreme Courts
to alter sentence on appeal.

Sentence review in Maine: comparisons and comments. Maine
Law Review 18 (2): 133-54, 1966
"In creating a specialized sentence-review
tribunal, Maine has instituted a simple and
inexpensive method for correcting the occa-
sional injustice."

Illinois Judicial Conference. Executive Committee
1962 annual report. 143p Chicago, Burdette Smith Co., 1963
Report on appellate review of criminal sentences, p. 73-79.

Maryland.
[Laws of 1966, c. 288, provides for special courts to review sentences.]

Maryland. Judicial Conference
Judicial review of sentences in criminal cases; by Edward D.
E. Rollins and J. Gilbert Prendergast. [Transcript of six-
teenth Judicial Conference, 1961, p. 219-53]

Mayers, Lewis
Federal review of state convictions: the need for procedural
reappraisal. George Washington Law Review 34: 615-65, May
1966
Basic to: Federal review of state convictions; some proposals
for change. Judicature (American Judicature Society) 50:
168-71, January 1967.

Mueller, Gerhard O. W.
  Penology on appeal; appellate review of legal but excessive
  sentences. Vanderbilt Law Review 15: 671-97, June 1962
            Appendix A: Current law of fifty states
            and the District of Columbia on appel-
            late review of legal but excessive sen-
            tences.

Mueller, Gerhard O. W. and Griffiths, F. L. P., eds.
  Comparative criminal procedure. 252p New York, New York
  University Press, 1969
            Appellate review of legal but excessive
            sentences, p. 199-230.

Mueller, Gerhard O. W. and LePoole, Fre
  Appellate review of legal but excessive sentences: a compar-
  ative study. Vanderbilt Law Review 21: 411+, May 1968
  Reprinted: Congressional Record, March 13, 1969: S2860-66.

New Jersey. Supreme Court. Committee on Criminal Procedure
  Report. New Jersey Law Journal 84: 245+, May 11, 1961
            Concerning pleas, split trial in murder
            cases, appellate review of sentences.

New York University. School of Law. Comparative Criminal Law
  Project
  Appellate review of legal but excessive sentences; a comparative study by Gerhard O. W. Mueller and Fre LePoole. 35p
  (mim) (Memorandum no. 3) New York, 1966?

Penology--appellate review of criminal sentences. Notre Dame
  Lawyer 35: 298-301, March 1960
            Concerning Commonwealth v. Green, 151 A.
            2d 241 (1959).

Pennsylvania. University. School of Law. Biddle Law Library
  Materials relating to appellate review of sentences; bibliography on the appellate review of criminal sentences; compiled by the Staff. January 12, 1966
  Reprinted: U.S. Senate Committee on the Judiciary, Subcommittee on Improvement in Judicial Machinery, Appellate review of sentences, hearings on S. 2722, March 1966, p. 146-
  49.

Review of legal but excessive sentences in the federal courts.
  DePaul Law Review 10: 104-16, Autumn-Winter, 1960
            Concerning United States v. Wiley, 278 F.
            2d 500 (1960).

U.S. Congress. Senate
    S. 3914, to provide for appellate review of sentences imposed
    in criminal cases arising in the district courts of the United
    States; text; statement. Congressional Record, August 30,
    1960: 18318-23

    S. 1692, to provide for the appellate review of sentences im-
    posed in criminal cases arising in the district courts of the
    United States; text; statement. Congressional Record, April
    20, 1961: 6347-48
            Result of work of Senate National Peniten-
            tiaries Subcommittee.

    S. 823, to provide for appellate review of sentences imposed
    in criminal cases arising in the district courts of the United
    States; text; statement. Congressional Record, February 18,
    1963: 2397

    S. 2722, to provide for the appellate review of sentences im-
    posed in criminal cases arising in district courts of the
    United States; statement. Congressional Record, November 8,
    1965: A6285-86

U.S. Congress. Senate. Committee on the Judiciary. Subcommit-
    tee on Improvements in Judicial Machinery
    Appellate review of sentences; hearings on S. 2722, March
    1-2, 1966. 196p (89:2) Washington, D.C., 1966
            Includes: Report of Maryland Governor's
            Commission to Study Sentencing in Criminal
            Cases; Memorandum concerning Maryland leg-
            islative action on Governor's Commission
            proposal; Appellate review of legal but
            excessive sentences, by New York Univer-
            sity School of Law, Comparative Criminal
            Law Project.

U.S. Congress. Senate
    S. 1540, to provide for appellate review of sentences im-
    posed in criminal cases arising in district courts of the
    United States; statement. Congressional Record, April 13,
    1967: 9335-36

U.S. Congress. Senate. Committee on the Judiciary
    Appellate review of sentences; report to accompany S. 1540.
    10p (90:1, S.Rep. no. 372) Washington, D.C., June 28, 1967

U.S. Congress. Senate
    S. 1561, relating to appellate review of criminal sentencing;
    text; statement. Congressional Record, March 13, 1969:
    S2852-66

U.S. Court of Appeals for the Second Circuit
  Appellate review of sentences; a symposium at the Judicial
  Conference, Manchester, Vt., September 24, 1962. Federal
  Rules Decisions 32: 249-321, 1963
          Exhibit 1: Canadian law on the subject of
          appellate review of sentences;
          Exhibit 2: Checks and balances on sentencing
          discretion;
          Exhibit 3: Letter by James V. Bennett;
          Exhibit 4: Questionnaire concerning re-
          view of criminal sentences.
  Reprinted: U.S. Senate Committee on the Judiciary, Subcommit-
  tee on National Penitentiaries, The federal prison system--
  1964; hearings, January 22, 1964, p. 303-463.

Watkins, Thomas W.
  Appellate review of the sentencing process in Michigan. University of Detroit Law Journal 36: 356-79, February 1959

Weigel, Stanley A.
  Appellate revision of sentences: to make the punishment fit
  the crime. Stanford Law Review 20: 405-22, February 1968
          Concerning disparity and inequity in fed-
          eral sentencing.
  Reprinted: Congressional Record, March 13, 1969: S2854-60.

SENTENCING INSTITUTES FOR JUDGES

In the 85th Congress, the concern about sentence disparities led to the introduction on July 29, 1957 of H.J.Res. 424, to improve the administration of justice by authorizing the establishment of institutes and joint councils on sentencing for the development of standards and policies to be followed in the sentencing of persons convicted of offenses against the United States.

U.S. Congress. House. Committee on the Judiciary
Federal sentencing procedures. 165p (85:2, H.Com.Print) Washington, D.C., February 15, 1958
Responses to letter concerning three proposals concerning sentence disparities (H.J.Res. 424, H.J.Res. 425, and H.R. 8923).

Federal sentencing procedure; hearing on H.J.Res. 424, H.J.Res. 425 and H.R. 8923, before Subcommittee No. 3, April 30, 1958. 81p (85:2) (Serial no. 14) Washington, D.C., 1958
Reference notes on federal sentencing procedures, p. 55-67.

Improving the administration of justice by authorizing the Judicial Conference of the United States to establish institutes and joint councils on sentencing, to provide additional methods of sentencing; report to accompany H.J.Res. 424. 20p (85:2, H.Rep. no. 1946) Washington, D.C. June 23, 1958

U.S. Congress. House. Committee of Conference
Federal sentencing procedures; conference report to accompany H.J.Res. 424. 3p (85:2, H.Rep. no. 2579) Washington, D.C., August 13, 1958

U.S. Congress. Senate. Committee on the Judiciary
[To improve the administration of justice by authorizing the Judicial Conference of the United States to establish institutes and joint councils on sentencing; report to accompany H.J.Res. 424.] 20p (85:2, S.Rep. no. 2013) Washington, D.C., July 29, 1958

Federal sentencing--institutes and joint councils.
United States Code, Congressional and Administrative News (85:2) 1958, v. 2: 3891-906

Public Law 85-752, 85th Congress, H.J.Res. 424....
International Review of Criminal Policy (14):
149-50, April 1959

In July 1959, under the authority of Pub.L. 85-752, the Judicial Conference of the United States held a pilot institute on
sentencing at Boulder, Colo. Three categories of offenses were
considered at the institute--income tax violator, automobile
thief, and fraudulent offender.

Pilot sentencing institute. Journal of Criminal
Law... 50: 385-87, November-December 1959

Sharp, Louis J.
The pilot institute on sentencing. Federal
Probation 23: 9-11, December 1959

U.S. Judicial Conference of the United States
Pilot institute on sentencing, Boulder, July
16-17, 1959. Federal Rules Decisions 26 (4-
5): 232-383, 1961
Background and objectives of the
institute program; the legal framework of sentencing; sentencing the
income tax violator; sentencing the
auto thief; resources in the disposition of the offender; sentencing
the fraudulent offender.
Excerpt: The inequality of jail sentences,
by Emanuel Celler. New York County Lawyers'
Association, Bar Bulletin 17: 92-96, November-December 1959.
Excerpt: An expression of congressional in-
terest in the federal sentencing institute,
by Emanuel Celler. Federal Probation 24:
3-6, June 1960.

Other materials relating to federal sentencing institutes and
councils include the following--

Doyle, Richard F.
A sentencing council in operation; before 22d annual confer-
ence of federal judges of Sixth Judicial Circuit, Dearborn,
April 28, 1961. Federal Probation 25: 27-30, September 1961
Council inaugurated by judges of U.S.
District Court for Eastern District of
Michigan.

Federal judges of Second Circuit conduct sentencing institute
[New York City, May 7, 1960]. Federal Probation 24: 81,
June 1960

Five U.S. judicial circuits to hold sentencing institutes.
Federal Probation 25: 75, September 1961

Judicial Conference of the Ninth Circuit
    Reports of committees and resolutions to be submitted to the
    Judicial Conference, July 17-19, 1968, San Francisco. 93,64p
    (mim) [1968]
            Report of Committee on Probation, Senten-
            cing Institutes and Seminars, p. 78.

Kaufman, Irving R.
    Enlightened sentences through improved technique; before Sec-
    ond Circuit Sentencing Institute, New York City, May 5, 1962.
    Federal Probation 26: 3-10, September 1962
            Concerning supervised release, probation,
            equality of treatment, study prior to sen-
            tence, indeterminate sentence, split sen-
            tence, and appellate review of sentences.

Samuels, Gertrude
    The judges go back to school. New York Times Magazine, No-
    vember 6, 1966: 36-37+

Thomsen, Roszel C.
    Sentencing in income tax cases; before Judicial Conference
    of the First Circuit, September 7, 1961. Federal Probation
    26: 10-13, March 1962

U.S. Bureau of Prisons. Inmate Training and Treatment Staff
    Federal sentencing statute--after one year [P.L. 85-752].
    Its Progress Report 7: 1-8, July-September 1959

U.S. Congress. Senate. Committee on the Judiciary. Subcommit-
    tee on National Penitentiaries
    National penitentiaries; report. 27p (87:1, S.Rep. no.
    170) Washington, D.C., April 18, 1961

U.S. Judicial Conference of the United States
    Sentencing Institute--the Circuit Conference of the Ninth
    Judicial Circuit [Pebble Beach, Calif., July 8, 1960].
    Federal Rules Decisions 27: 287-391, 1961
            Juvenile delinquency, by William M. McCord;
            The new sentencing statutes from the pro-

bation officer's viewpoint, by Albert Wahl;
Must an adult prisoner committed for study
be returned to court for final sentencing,
by Louis E. Goodman;
Individualizing the sentence function, by
James V. Bennett.

U.S. Judicial Conference of the United States
  Sentencing Institute and Joint Council for the Fifth Circuit
  [New Orleans, May 9-10, 1961]. Federal Rules Decisions 30:
  185-328, 1962
  Legislative views as to the value of the
  Institute, by Emanuel Celler;
  The presentence report, by Louis J. Sharp;
  Utilization of the presentence report and
  other presentence resources, by Bryan Simp-
  son;
  What can a judge do with an adult defendant,
  by Seybourn H. Lynne;
  With a juvenile delinquent, a youth offen-
  der or a young adult offender, by Frank M.
  Johnson;
  How the Federal Bureau of Investigation
  feels about the relationship of sentences
  and law enforcement, by Cartha D. DeLoach;
  Sentencing the auto thief, by Walter E.
  Hoffman, Benjamin C. Dawkins, Jr., and
  Joe E. Estes;
  Sentencing the fraudulent offender, by
  William A. Bootle and Allen B. Hannay;
  The offender who violates both federal and
  state law, by Edward F. Hunter, Jr.;
  Sentencing the income tax violator, by
  J. Skelly Wright, Harlan H. Grooms, Wil-
  liam E. Miller, and Daniel H. Thomas;
  Would a system where sentences are fixed
  by a board of experts be preferable? by
  Louis E. Goodman;
  Summary and evaluation of the Institute,
  by Ben C. Connally.

Seminar and Institute on Disparity of Sentences for Sixth,
Seventh and Eighth Judicial Circuits [Highland Park, October 12-13, 1961]. Federal Rules Decisions 30: 401-505,
1962
  Workshops: presentence information, commitments for diagnosis, probation or incarceration, personality and background
  characteristics of the offender.
  Objectives of the Institute, by Edwin A.
  Robson;

Legislative views on the importance of the
Sentencing Institute, by Emanuel Celler;
Relationship of criminal sentences to law
enforcement, by Cartha D. DeLoach;
Presentence resources, by Louis J. Sharp;
New sentencing procedures available to
federal courts, by James V. Bennett;
[Justice is found in the hearts and minds
of free men], by Robert F. Kennedy.
Excerpt: Justice is found in the hearts and minds of free
men, by Robert F. Kennedy. Federal Probation 25: 3-5, De-
cember 1961.
Comment: 84 federal judges attend Sentencing Institute.
Federal Probation 25: 76, December 1961.
Comment: The Highland Park Institute on Sentence Disparity,
by Frank J. Remington and Donald J. Newman. Federal Probation 26: 3-9, March 1962.

U.S. Judicial Conference of the United States
Institute on Sentencing for United States District Judges
[Denver, February 1964]. Federal Rules Decisions 35: 381-
99, October 1964
Remarks, by Luther W. Youngdahl;
Trends in sentencing since 1957 and areas
of substantial agreement, by Francis L.
Van Dusen;
Aids in sentencing, by James B. Parsons;
Application of psychiatry to study obser-
vation and treatment of the federal of-
fender, by John W. Oliver;
The medical center for federal prisoners,
by Russell O. Settle;
When and how should a sentencing judge use
probation, by William B. Herlands.

Judicial Institute on Sentencing, February 1-8, 1964--ref-
erence data. 15pts Washington, D.C., n.d.
Includes: Suggested guidelines for the
study of defendants under 18 U.S.C. 4208
(b), by Federal Bureau of Prisons, January 1964.

Institutes on Sentencing for United States District Judges
[Lompoc, Calif, October 22, 1964, Lewisburg, Pa., November
11-13, 1964]. Federal Rules Decisions 37: 111-214, 1965
Basic sentencing philosophies, by Harry
C. Westover;
Some guidelines in preparing presentence
reports, by Victor Evjen;
Jail sentences in anti-trust cases, by
Robert L. Wright;

Comments on various sentencing situations,
by Eugene N. Barkin;
Mental health and criminal behavior, by
Philip Q. Roche;
Federal parole, by Richard A. Chappell.

U.S. Judicial Conference of the United States
Sentencing Institute of the Ninth Circuit [McNeil Island
and Lakewood Center, September 1965]. Federal Rules Decisions 39: 523-66, 1966
Sentencing problems, by Eugene N. Barkin;
Of judicial hearings to determine mental
competency to stand trial, by John W. Oliver;
Psychiatric approaches to the mentally ill
federal offender, by Charles E. Smith.

U.S. Court of Appeals for the Second Circuit
Sentencing Institute [New York, November 11, 1966]. Federal
Rules Decisions 41: 467-517, 1966
Sentencing procedure in the United States
District Court for the Eastern District of
New York, by Joseph C. Zavatt;
Impact of recent legislation and rule
changes upon sentencing, by Eugene N.
Barkin;
Federal sentencing problems and the Model
Sentencing Act, by Sol Rubin.

U.S. Court of Appeals for the Tenth Circuit
Institute of Sentencing for United States Judges of the
Eighth and Tenth Judicial Circuits [Denver, July 11-13,
1966]. Federal Rules Decisions 41: 249-56, 42: 175-233,
1967
How can we effectively minimize unjusti-
fied disparity in federal criminal sentences? by Edward J. Devitt;
Identification of the dangerous offender,
by Howard P. Rome;
Objectivity in predicting criminal behavior, by Richard A. McGee;
Treatment of the nondangerous offender,
by Merrill A. Smith;
Sentences must be rationally explained,
by Sol Rubin.

U.S. Court of Appeals for the Fourth and Fifth Circuits
Institute on Sentencing [Atlanta, October 30-31, 1967].
Federal Rules Decisions 45: 149-98, 1969
Rule 11 and the plea of guilty, by Walter
E. Hoffman;

Requirements of Rules 11 and 14 of the
Federal Rules of Criminal Procedure, by
Ewin M. Stanley;
The dangerous offender under the Model
Sentencing Act, by Alfred P. Murrah;
Sentencing the dangerous offender,
Roszel C. Thomsen;
Some aspects of federal probation with
emphasis on the work of the probation of-
ficers and the discussions between the
sentencing judge and the probation offi-
cer prior to sentencing, by Francis L.
Van Dusen;
Politics and pragmatism in crime control,
by Norval Morris.
Excerpt: Sentencing the dangerous offender, by Roszel C.
Thomsen. Federal Probation 32: 3-4, March 1968.
Excerpt: The dangerous offender under the Model Sentencing
Act, by Alfred P. Murrah. Federal Probation 32: 3-9, June
1968.
Excerpt: Politics and pragmatism in crime control, by Nor-
val Morris. Federal Probation 32: 9-16, June 1968.

In recent years, several states have been concerned with educa-
tion of judges.

Hudson, Eugene A.
    Should sentencing institutes be established?
    American Trial Lawyer 3: 11-12, December-Janu-
    ary 1966-67

Institute of Judicial Administration
    Judicial education in the United States; a sur-
    vey. 276p (mim) New York, July 15, 1965

Parker, Graham E.
    The education of the sentencing judge. Inter-
    national and Comparative Law Quarterly s4, 14:
    206-51, January 1965

California

California. Judicial Council
    Proceedings of the...Sentencing Institute for Superior Court
    Judges, no. 1, March 1965-no. 5, March 1969. 5nos San Fran-
    cisco, 1965-69
            Institutes authorized by California Laws
        of 1963, c. 2075.

California. Judicial Council
   Proceedings of the third annual Institute for Juvenile Court
   Judges and Referees, May 14-15, 1964. 226p (process) San
   Francisco, 1964
         It's the judges decision, or is it? by
         Joseph D. Lohman and others.

   Proceedings of the [fourth] annual Institute for Juvenile
   Court Judges and Referees, May 13-14, 1966. 170p San Francisco 1966
         The disposition decision: relevant factors
         and considerations, p. 100-38.

   Proceedings of the Institute for Municipal and Justice Court
   Judges, 1964, 1966-1968. 4nos San Francisco, 1964-68
         Includes: Sentencing the offender, standards
         and significant factors.

   Proceedings of the 1966 and 1967 workshops for presiding
   judges of the metropolitan municipal courts, June 10, 1966
   and February 17, 1967. 71,42p San Francisco, 1967
         Includes: Disparities in sentencing.

Indiana

Indiana Citizens Council on Crime and Delinquency
   [Fourth Annual Institute of Judges, Wabash College, August
   22-24, 1963.] Indianapolis, 1963
         The Model Sentencing Act, by Sol Rubin;
         Constitutional rights in criminal trials,
         by John M. Lewis.

   [Fifth Annual Institute of Judges, Wabash College, August
   20-24, 1964.] Indianapolis, 1964
         Judges institutes and seminars, their
         uses and effects, by Sol Rubin.

North Carolina

Conference of Superior Court Judges of North Carolina and
   Others
   Superior Court Judges Seminar [University of North Carolina,
   June 1964]; [notes submitted by different judges suggesting
   methods for the more effective administration of justice].
   n.p. (mim) Chapel Hill, University of North Carolina,
   Institute of Government, 1964
   Comment: Popular Government (University of North Carolina)
   31: 21, September 1964.
         Includes: Sentencing and probation.

Pennsylvania

Crime Commission of Philadelphia
First Philadelphia Judicial Sentencing Institute [Valley
Forge, October 29-30, 1965]. Federal Rules Decisions 40:
399-477, 1966
Sentencing and law enforcement, by J. Ed-
ward Lumbard;
Mental health and criminal behavior, by
Melvin Heller;
Aids in sentencing, by John Wallace:
Treatment resources in prisons and jails,
by Frank Loveland.
Comment: Pennsylvania Association on Probation, Parole and
Correction, Quarterly 22: 44-45, Winter 1965.

[Western Pennsylvania Sentencing Institute, Ligonier, June
10-11, 1966.] Its News 6: 4, June 1966
Comment: Judges study sentencing techniques at Institute,
by Samuel J. Feigus. Trial Judges' Journal 5: 2, October
1966.

[Third Judicial Sentencing Institute, Allentown, December
2-3, 1966.] Its News 6: 1+, October 1966

Fourth Judicial Sentencing Institute [Bedford, June 20-21,
1968]. Federal Rules Decisions 46: 497-604, 1969
Sentencing Institute--substance and proc-
ess, by Ephraim R. Gomberg;
Responsibility and mental competence, by
David L. Bazelon;
Sentencing innovations, by Herbert Wechsler;
Violence and its relation to sentencing,
by Marvin E. Wolfgang;
The violent criminal, by Hans H. Toch;
Dangerousness, diagnosis and disposition,
by Melvin S. Heller.

Laub, Burton R.
The man on the bench--observations on sentencing procedures;
before Philadelphia Crime Commission Judicial Conference,
Allentown, December 2, 1966. Pennsylvania Bar Association,
Quarterly 40: 129-35, October 1968

SENTENCING IN THE STATES

Since 1954, an annual analysis of state legislation and court cases in the field of corrections has been published in the NPPA Journal and Crime and Delinquency. Sentencing is included in the analysis.

> Rubin, Sol
> Developments in correctional law. Crime and
> Delinquency 16: 185-97, April 1970
> > Includes: Presentence investigation and
> > the hearing on the sentence; prison terms
> > longer than the minimum for the crime;
> > increased sentence after retrial.

> U.S. Library of Congress. American Law Division
> List of states which provide that persons
> found guilty shall be punished by death or
> by life imprisonment without possibility of
> parole for certain criminal offenses.
> Reprinted: Congressional Record, March 1,
> 1962: 3306.
>
> States, criminal offenses on which capital pun-
> ishment is imposed. February 27, 1962
> Reprinted: Congressional Record, March 1,
> 1962: 3300-04.

> U.S. Library of Congress. Legislative Reference
> Service
> Compilation of District of Columbia and state
> criminal statistics showing a comparison of
> mandatory minimum and maximum sentences that
> can be imposed; by Ruth H. Stromberg and others.
> January 17, 1964
> Reprinted: U.S. Senate Committee on the District
> of Columbia, Crime in the District of Columbia,
> hearings, April 27-August 5, 1965, pt. 1, p. 157-
> 208, 1965.

Materials relating to sentencing in particular states include the following--

Alaska

Alaska. Judicial Council
First annual report, 1960. 12p+ (process) Anchorage,
January 1961
> Includes: Recommendation to extend author-

ity to magistrates to suspend all or a
portion of the sentence in a criminal
case.

Fifth report, 1967-1968. 56p (mim) Anchorage, January
1969
Report of December 12-13, 1968 meeting in
Sitka, a sentencing conference, p. 33-35;
Report on Alaska Court System Sentencing
Institute for Superior Court Judges, Ketch-
ikan, May 17, 1968, p. 53-54.

Alaska. Legislative Council. Legislative Affairs Agency
Criminal penalties under the Alaska criminal code. 101p
(mim) Juneau, January 1969

Rehbock, Ernest Z.
Sentence appeals in perspective: the Alaska way. Judicature 54: 156-61, November 1970
Sitka Sentence Seminar conferees expressed
a preference for an inexpensive sentence
appeal which would result in gradually developing sentencing criteria in Supreme
Court opinions.

California

California. Department of Justice. Bureau of Criminal Statistics
The influence of offense upon the administration of juvenile justice; by R. James Rasmussen. 7p (process) Sacramento, November 1966
Concerning an examination of juvenile probation department determinations and juvenile court dispositions in relation to the
offense alleged and/or sustained.

California. Legislature. Assembly. Interim Committee on Crim-
inal Procedure
Deterrent effects of criminal sanctions; progress report.
71p Sacramento, May 1968
Pt. 1: Public knowledge of criminal pen-
alties; a research report, by Social Psy-
chiatry Research Associates, San Francisco,
February 1968.
Pt. 2: Crime and penalties in California,
by Assembly Office of Research, March 1968.
Pt. 3: Request for proposals, by Assembly
Office of Research, Spring 1968.
Same: California Assembly, Appendix to the Journal of the
Assembly, Supplement, 1968.

California. Legislature. Assembly. Office of Research
   Crime and penalties in California. 124p (process) Sacramento, March 1968

California. Legislature. Joint Committee for Revision of the
   Penal Code
   Basic felony sentencing provisions; proposed tentative draft
   and commentary; by Sanford H. Kadish. 36p Berkeley, University of California, School of Law, Project Office, 1967

   Penal code revision project, tentative draft no. 2. 188p
   Berkeley, University of California, School of Law, Project
   Office, June 1968
        Includes: Disposition of offenders.

   Sentencing: extended terms; draft 2, by Herbert L. Packer.
   3p Berkeley, University of California, School of Law, Project Office, 1966

California College of Trial Judges
   Criminal proceedings; sentencing and probation; by Lewis
   Drucker. looseleaf Berkeley, University of California,
   Earl Warren Legal Center, 1967

Criminal Courts Bar Association of Los Angeles
   Seminar on criminal law and procedure, March 16, 1963; program. 51p Los Angeles, 1963
        Probation and sentence, by Evelle J.
        Younger, p. 16-19.

   Seminar on criminal law and procedure. ed.2 60p Los Angeles
   1964
        Sentencing, post conviction procedures,
        by Lewis Drucker, p. 56-60.

The cruel and unusual punishment clause and the substantive
   criminal law. Harvard Law Review 79: 635-55, January 1966
        Concerning Robinson v. California, 370 U.S.
        660 (1962).

McDonald, D.J.
   New legal lights in corrections. Correctional Review (California Department of Corrections), September 1964: 8-13
        Includes: Sentencing.

National Council on Crime and Delinquency
   The California sentencing law; by Sol Rubin. 22p New York,
   April 1964

Sentencing criminals in California--a study in haphazard legislation. Stanford Law Review 13: 340-65, March 1961
        Includes: Probation, concurrent and conse-
        cutive sentences, additional fine, court's
        discretion in treatment of sexual psycho-
        path.

Swain, Frank G.
    Salvage material in our criminal courts. Fortnight 20: 41-
42+, April 1957
        Concerning interviews between judge and
        defendant before and after sentencing.

Colorado

Colorado. Legislative Council
    Colorado criminal law; report to the Colorado General Assem-
    bly. 166p (process) (Research publication no. 68) Denver,
    December 1962
        Sentencing, p. 1-36.

Colorado's programs in the field of corrections; report to
the Colorado General Assembly. 129p (process) (Research
report no. 21) Denver, December 1956
        Sentencing practices, p. 93-96.

Progress reports on children's laws, migratory labor, criminal code--sentencing. 51p (process) (Research publication
no. 59) Denver, December 1961
        Sentencing criminal offenders, p. 29-48.

Connecticut

Connecticut. Commission to Revise the Criminal Statutes
    Report, [1967]. 141p Hartford, [1967]
        Includes: Authorized disposition of of-
        fenders, sentences of probation, condi-
        tional discharge and unconditional dis-
        charge, sentences of imprisonment.

Connecticut. Governor's Committee on Gambling
    Second, third and fourth reports. 23p Hartford, [1969]
        Deterrent effect of jail sentences, p. 13;
        Court sentencing, p. 15.

Florida

Florida. State University
    The impact of the Gideon decision upon crime and sentencing

in Florida: a study of recidivism and sociocultural change;
by Charles J. Eichman. Thesis (M.S.), December 1965
> "Florida judges have not become signifi-
> cantly more prone to use incarceration in
> disposing of felony cases since the Gideon
> decision."

Reprinted: (Research monograph no. 2) Tallahassee, Florida
Divison of Corrections, Research and Statistics Section,
October 1966.

Gattis, Donald J., Jr.
Judgment and sentence in a Florida criminal case. University of Florida Law Review 16: 312-28, Fall 1963

Georgia

Atlanta, Ga. Commission on Crime and Juvenile Delinquency
Opportunity for urban excellence. 129p 1966
> Crime prevention and sentencing, p. 159-
> 70.

Georgia Citizens Committee on Crime and Delinquency
Partners in crime control; by Robert M. Hill, before meeting of March 17, 1964. 8p (mim) Atlanta, 1964
> Concerning sentencing practices.

Georgia. University. Institute of Law and Government
Summary of Georgia Appellate Court decisions which affect
local government, September 1963-September 1964: by R. P.
Sentell, Jr. 36p Athens, September 1964
> Includes: Jail sentence.

Molnar, T. T.
Criminal law revision in Georgia. Mercer Law Review 15:
399-430, Spring 1964
> Concerning Illinois and Georgia sentencing
> procedures in death penalty cases.

Illinois

Illinois State and Chicago Bar Associations. Joint Committee
to Revise the Illinois Criminal Code
Tentative final draft of the proposed Illinois Code of Criminal Procedure. 155p Chicago, Burdette Smith, December 1962
> Art.54: Sentence and judgment;
> Art.55: Execution of sentence.

A new revised criminal code for Illinois. American Judicature
Society, Journal 44: 159, January 1961
> Concerning change in code that allows
> trial judge, not jury, to pass sentence.

Starrs, James E.
  The post-conviction hearing act--1949-60 and beyond. DePaul
  Law Review 10: 397-412, Spring-Summer 1961

Wexler, Morris J.
  The disposition of criminal cases [especially in Cook County
  courts]. Chicago Bar Record 37: 313-16, April 1956

Indiana

Indiana. General Assembly. Legislative Advisory Commission
  Report to the General Assembly of 1965. 327p Indianapolis,
  November 1964
          Report of Committee to Study State Laws
          Pertaining to Criminal Offenses, Penalties
          and Procedures, p. 17-32.

  Biennial report to the 95th General Assembly, November 1966.
  473p Indianapolis, 1967
          Report of Committee to Study State Laws
          Pertaining to Criminal Offenses, Penalties
          and Procedures, p. 77-100.

Iowa

Criminal sentence revision--a necessity. Iowa Law Review 49:
  499-515, Winter 1964

Iowa. State College. Department of Economics and Sociology
  The courts and criminal justice in Iowa; by Walter A. Lunden. 133p (process) Ames, 1957
          Includes: Inequalities in sentencing
          practices.

Lunden, Walter A.
  Felons in Iowa courts. Presidio (Iowa State Penitentiary)
  31: 20-23, February 1965
          Concerning imposition of prison sentences
          by district courts.
  Abstract: International Bibliography on Crime and Delinquency 3: 47, July 1965.

  A quarter century of criminal justice in Iowa. 17p (process) Ames, Iowa State University of Science and Technology,
  1959
          Includes: Disposition of criminal cases
          (use of jail and fines).
          Prepared for Iowa Governor's Committee on

Penal Affairs and Iowa Correction Congress,
September 8, 1959.
Comment: Journal of Criminal Law... 50: 387-88, November-
December 1959.

Kentucky

Kentucky. Legislative Research Commission
Kentucky statutes: criminal penalties; by Norman W. Lawson,
Jr. 199p (process) (Informational bulletin no. 69) Frank-
fort, March 1969

Palmore, John S.
After the verdict: the problem of sentencing and corrections
in Kentucky. Kentucky State Bar Journal 26: 32-45, January
1962

Louisiana

Louisiana. State Law Institute
Title XXX. Sentence. 51p (Code of criminal procedure re-
vision, expose des motifs no. 27) Baton Rouge, March 1965
C. 2: Suspended sentence and probation.

Maryland

Maryland. Governor's Commission to Study Sentencing in Criminal Cases
[Final] report, December 17, 1965. 40p Baltimore, 1965
Reprinted: U.S. Senate Committee on the Judiciary, Subcommittee on Improvements in Judicial Machinery, Appellate review of sentences; hearings on S. 2722, March 1966, p. 155-
95.

Maryland State Bar Association. Committee on Review of Criminal Sentences
Report. Its Transactions, 1962: 344-62. Baltimore, 1962

Massachusetts

Massachusetts. Judicial Council
Forty-first report, 1965. 80p (Public document no. 144)
Boston, 1966
Includes: Minimum sentence for persons
convicted of certain auto crimes.

Forty-fourth report, 1968. 145p (Public document no. 144)
Boston, 1968
Includes: Discretion in sentencing.

Massachusetts. Parole Board
  Special report...relative to the feasibility of changing the
  law relative to the mandatory time to be served by prisoners
  convicted of certain gambling offenses.... 25p (House no.
  3350) Boston, January 1963

Michigan

Coffey, Thomas L.
  Recidivism and court disposition. Thesis (M._), University
  of Michigan, School of Social Work, 1961
          Study of court sentences given adult of-
          fenders in Saginaw, Mich.
  Abstract: International Bibliography on Crime and Delinquency 3: 56, August 1965.

Gilmore, Horace W.
  Responsibility in sentencing. Trial Judges' Journal 5: 1+,
  January 1966
          In Michigan, an eight-judge sentencing
          panel determines sentences in the dis-
          trict court.

Jaros, Dean and Mendelsohn, Robert I.
  The judicial role and sentencing behavior. Midwest Journal
  of Political Science 11: 471-88, November 1967
          Based on data gathered by direct observa-
          tion of Detroit Traffic Court, Summer 1966.

Michigan Crime and Delinquency Council and Michigan Corrections
  Commission
  Conference proceedings from "conference on sentencing," Lan-
  sing, December 5, 1966. 87p East Lansing, 1967
          The need for sentencing reform, by Thomas
          M. Kavanagh;
          A rational approach to sentencing reform,
          by Sol Rubin:
          Sentencing nondangerous offenders, by Eu-
          gene N. Barkin;
          Sentencing dangerous offenders, by Ralph
          Brancale;
          Sentencing persons in organized crime;
          a panel.

Michigan State Bar. Committee on Sentence, Probation and
  Parole
  Sentence, probation and parole. Michigan State Bar Journal
  44: 69-71, September 1965

National Council on Crime and Delinquency
   The Michigan sentencing and penal laws; a report to the Committee on Criminal Jurisprudence of the State Bar of Michigan. 45p (mim) New York, 1961

Minnesota

Bauer, Barton O. and Others
   A study of the variations in the length of sentences given
   adult, male, felony offenders in the state of Minnesota.
   Thesis (M._), University of Minnesota, School of Social Work,
   June 1961

Minnesota. Department of Corrections
   Limited versus maximum felony sentences imposed by district
   courts in Minnesota: Study 2, January 1-December 31, 1964;
   by Nathan G. Mandel and F. T. Telander. 10p (mim) St. Paul,
   May 1965
            Study of 1964 commitments at State Reform-
            atory for Men and the Minnesota State Prison.
   Abstract: International Bibliography on Crime and Delinquency 3: 111-12, October 1965.

Minnesota. Governor's Commission on Law Enforcement, Administration of Justice and Corrections
   Report of Committee on Administration of Justice. v.p.
   (mim) St. Paul, January 22, 1968
            Includes: Disparate sentences.

Missouri

Reiter, Robert E.
   A review of sentencing in Missouri: the need for re-evalua-
   tion- and change. St. Louis University Law Journal 11: 69-
   82, Fall 1966

New Jersey

Essex County Bar Association
   Some thoughts on criminal correction; by Arthur S. Lane.
   13p (mim) January 12, 1965
   Abstract: International Bibliography on Crime and Delinquency 3: 191, October 1965.

New Jersey. Administrative Office of the Courts
   Supplement to sentencing manual for judges. 16p+ Trenton,
   1970

New Jersey. Supreme Court. Committee on Sentencing Problems
   Report. 5p (mim) Trenton, February 27, 1957
            Includes: Report on the Rhode Island de-
            ferred sentence procedure, by Edward Gaul-
            kin.

Urbaniak, Eugene T.
   The legal effect of criminal sentences in New Jersey. Wel-
   fare Reporter (New Jersey Department of Institutions and
   Agencies) 10: 122-30, July 1959
            Includes: Type of sentence, consecutive
            sentence, jail time credit.

New York State

Correctional Association of New York
   Recommendations to the 1970 Legislature. Its Newsletter 4:
   1+, January 1970
            Includes: State control over sentenced
            offenders.

National Council on Crime and Delinquency. New York Citizen
   Council
   Position statement on the proposed New York penal law; by
   Cornelius W. Wickersham, Jr. before Temporary Commission on
   Revision of the Penal Law and Criminal Code. 16p (mim)
   New York, November 1964
   Abstract: International Bibliography on Crime and Delin-
   quency 3: 58-59, September 1965.

New York City, N.Y. Parole Commission
   A critical review of a recommendation in the proposed New
   York penal law and the danger of its limiting the adminis-
   tration of criminal justice in the city of New York; by
   John J. Quinn. 8p (mim) August 1964
            Concerning definite sentencing and parole
            of prisoners.

[New York City and Kings County, N.Y. Criminal Court]
   [Uniformity in sentencing is aim of experimental system
   which separates trial from sentence.] American Judicature
   Society, Journal 59: 73, August 1965

New York State. Law Revision Commission
   Act, recommendation and study relating to extraordinary proceedings for review of conviction of sentence in a criminal
   action. p.425-88 (Legislative document (1959) no. 65(L))
   Albany, 1959

   Act, recommendation and study relating to extraordinary proceedings for review of conviction or sentence in a criminal

action or in certain criminal proceedings. 46p (Legislative
document (1960) no. 65 (H)) Albany, 1960
Comment: Code of Criminal Procedure: proposed sections...
extraordinary proceedings for a review of conviction or
sentence in a criminal action or in certain criminal proceedings. Albany Law Review 24: 480-85, June 1960.

New York State. Law Revision Commission
　Report. 23p (Legislative document (1960) no. 65) Albany,
　February 1, 1960
　　　　　Includes: Extraordinary proceedings for a
　　　　　review of conviction or sentence in a crimi-
　　　　　nal action.

New York State. Temporary Commission on Revision of the Penal
　and Criminal Code
　Interim report, February 1, 1963. 73p (Legislative docu-
　ment (1963) no. 8) Albany, 1963
　　　　　"High mandatory minimum sentences tie the
　　　　　hands of the courts and probation officers
　　　　　in determining a sentence tailored to the
　　　　　circumstances of the offense and the char-
　　　　　acter of the individual defendant."

　Fifth interim report, February 1, 1966. 47p (Legislative
　document (1966) no. 28) Albany, 1966
　　　　　Sentencing, p. 22-25.

　Proposed New York criminal procedure law; 1968 study bill
　and commission report. 307p Mineola, N.Y. Edward Thompson
　Co., September 1968
　　　　　Sentence, p. 141-59.

North Carolina

Ashman, Allan
　The General Assembly and the decision to sentence; before
　fifth annual seminar of North Carolina Superior Court Judges,
　June 17, 1968. Popular Government (University of North Car-
　olina, Institute of Government) 35: 9-17, September 1968
　　　　　Includes: Sentencing for public drunkenness
　　　　　and chronic alcoholism.

Gill, Douglas R.
　Legal problems in "punishment." Popular Government (Univer-
　sity of North Carolina, Institute of Government) 32: 11+,
　February 1966

Hall, Roy G., Jr.
　Criminal procedure. Popular Government (University of North
　Carolina, Institute of Government) 25: 62-65, June 1959

Smith, Weldon J.
    Unconstitutional judicial sentences. Washington and Lee Law
    Review 21: 343-45, Fall 1964
            Concerning State v. Blackmon, 132 S.E. 2d
        880 (1963).

Ohio

Ohio Legal Center Institute. Juvenile Court Judges Training
    Program
    The disposition process; by John J. Mayer, before Juvenile
    Court Judges Seminar, 1963, p. 1-11
    Abstract: Crime and Delinquency Abstracts 4 (2): 204, 1966.

Oregon

Beckett, William A.
    Criminal penalties in Oregon. Oregon Law Review 40: 1-195,
    December 1960-February 1961

Oregon. State Board of Control
    A balanced correctional system for Oregon; a survey by the
    National Council on Crime and Delinquency. v.p. (process)
    Salem, 1966
            C. 6: A statistical look at sentencing.

Pennsylvania

Gernert, Paul J.
    Study of sentences imposed for new offenses committed while
    on parole. Pennsylvania Chiefs of Police Association, Bul-
    letin 25: 13+, Winter 1966

Green, Edward
    An analysis of the sentencing practices of criminal court
    judges in Philadelphia. Thesis (Ph.D.), University of Penn-
    sylvania, 1959
            Based on court and police records in Phila-
            delphia, 1956-1957.
    Same: (Microfilm AC-1, no. 59-2234) Ann Arbor, University
    Microfilms, 1959.
    Similar title: American Journal of Correction 22: 32-35,
    July-August 1960.

    Judicial attitudes in sentencing; a study of the factors un-
    derlying the sentencing practice of the Criminal Court of
    Philadelphia. 149p (Cambridge studies in criminology v. 15)
    London, Macmillan, 1961

Kessler, Nathan
  Anomalous penalties in the criminal law of Pennsylvania. Villanova Law Review 3: 142-55, January 1958
        Concerning license and health law viola-
        tions; nonuniformity of penalties; con-
        flicting penalties for similar offenses;
        penalties for larceny and burglary; stat-
        utory omissions.

Pennsylvania. Board of Parole
  A study of types of sentences; by William L. Jacks.   5p (mim)
  Harrisburg, March 6, 1964
        Concerning a study of parolees released
        during 1960-61.

Pennsylvania. General Assembly. Joint State Government Commission
  Proposed crimes code for Pennsylvania.   226p Harrisburg,
  1967
        Art. VI, authorized disposition of offenders;
        Art. VII, authority of court in sentencing.

Pennsylvania Association on Probation, Parole and Correction
  Needed legislation in the field of crime and delinquency;
  workshop no. 11, annual conference, May 26, 1964. Its Quarterly 21: 51-57, June 1964
        Concerning statutory minimum sentence, and
        mandatory presentence investigations in all
        cases involving bodily harm to victim.

  Proceedings of the regional conference of the Southcentral
  Area Council of PAPPC, Johnstown, November 5-6, 1964. Its
  Quarterly 21: 24-29, December 1964
        Presentence investigation and report, by
        Harold W. Kelton;
        Sentence of the defendant, by Loran L.
        Lewis.

Pennsylvania State Bar Association. Committee on Criminal Law
  Recodification and the Model Penal Code
  Draft report to Joint State Government Commission.   29p (mim)
  Harrisburg, July 15, 1963
        Pt. 3: Treatment and correction (limiting
        the variety of possible sentences, extend-
        ed terms for persistent offenders, setting
        the maximum in individual sentences, judi-
        cial control of minimum, mandatory parole
        component in felony sentences, judicial
        discretion to sentence).

Philadelphia finds court reorganization problematic. Judicature 53: 167-68, November 1969
            Judges will not adopt any generalized
            policy of sentencing but will dispose of
            each case on its merits and the evidence
            before them.

Tennessee

Tennessee. Law Revision Commission
   Authorized disposition of offenders; a comparison of Ten-
   nessee and other provisions. 188p (Work document 38-5(1)
   Criminal Code) Nashville, June 1970
            Title 38, C. 5: Authorized disposition of
            offenders.

Court authority in sentencing; comparison of Tennessee and
   other provisions. 142p (Work document 38-6(1) Criminal
   Code) Nashville, June 1970
            Title 38, C. 6: Court authority in sentenc-
            ing.

Texas

Baab, George W. and Furgeson, William R., Jr.
   Texas sentencing practices: a statistical study. Texas Law
   Review 45: 471-503, February 1962
            Study of 1,720 cases from 27 courts in 19
            counties located in 4 geographical areas
            of Texas.

Virginia

Virginia. Advisory Legislative Council
   Revision of the recidivist statutes and related matters; report. 23p Richmond, 1967
            Concerning feasibility of placing authority
            to sentence convicted felons in hands of
            judges, removing such authority from jury.

Wisconsin

Babst, Dean V. and Mannering, John W.
   Probation versus imprisonment for similar types of offenders;
   a comparison by subsequent violations. Journal of Research
   in Crime and Delinquency 2: 60-71, July 1965
            Study of 7,614 Wisconsin cases--male of-
            fenders imprisoned compared with those
            placed on probation for similar offenses.

Bardwell, Richard W.
   Sentencing alternatives under Wisconsin law; before State
   Judicial Conference, January 1970. Wisconsin Bar Bulletin
   43: 18-20+, April 1970

SENTENCING IN THE FEDERAL COURTS

"The sentencing categories in present federal law are chaotic
and inconsistent. Very similar crimes have widely disparate
sentences."

> U.S. National Commission on Reform of Federal
>   Criminal Laws
>   Study draft of a new federal criminal code
>   (Title 18, United States Code). 344p Washing-
> ton, D.C., 1970
>   Pt. C: The sentencing system.
> Comment: Sentencing under the draft federal code,
> by Edmund G. Brown and Louis B. Schwartz. Ameri-
> can Bar Association, Journal 56: 935-40, October
> 1970.
>
> Working papers. 2v Washington, D.C., July 1970
>   V. 2, p. 1289-337: Comment on the senten-
>   cing system, by Peter W. Low.
>
> Memorandum on sentencing structure for the federal
> penal code. 117p Washington, D.C., 1968
>
> Final report. 366p Washington, D.C., January
> 1971

Materials relating to sentencing in the federal courts include
the following--

Bowman, Joseph M.
    Processing a motion attacking sentence under Section 2255 of
    the Judicial Code [28 U.S.C. §2255 (1958)]. University of
    Pennsylvania Law Review 111: 788-819, April 1963

Byrne, William M., Jr.
    Federal sentencing procedures: need for reform. Los Angeles
    Bar Bulletin 42: 563-67, October 1967
        Concerning disparity of sentences.

Cannon, Joe A. and Others
    Law and tactics in sentencing. 201p Washington, D.C.,
    Coiner Publications, 1970
            Study of federal sentencing process by
            E. Barrett Prettyman Fellows, Georgetown
            University Law Center.

Carter, James M. and Kunzel, Fred
Forms of adjudication for use in sentencing. Federal Rules
Decisions 44: 197-223, 1968

Chappell, Richard A.
Disparity in federal sentencing; before National Association
of Municipal Judges, Montreal, October 5, 1965. Municipal
Court Review 6: 18-20, April 1966
         Concerning sentencing councils and insti-
         tutes.

Craig, Walter E.
Sentencing in federal tax fraud cases; before Institute on
Defending Tax Fraud Prosecutions of the Practising Law Institute, Las Vegas, December 12-13, 1969. Federal Rules Decisions 49: 97-115, 1970

Criminal procedure--Federal Court of Appeals vacates sentence
on grounds of severity and remands to district court for
sentencing. University of Pennsylvania Law Review 109: 422-
28, January 1961
         Concerning United States v. Wiley, 278 F. 2d
         500 (1960).

Devitt, Edward J.
Improvements in federal sentencing procedures; before Judi-
cial Conference of Eighth Circuit, Duluth, July 20-29, 1959.
Federal Rules Decisions 24: 147-54, 1959

80 percent of the sentencing recommendations for 327 federal
prisoners. American Judicature Society, Journal 45: 106,
October 1961
         Concerning 1960 report of Federal Bureau
         of Prisons.

Federal Rules of Criminal Procedure--right to have illegal
sentence corrected under Rule 35. University of Detroit Law
Journal 39: 599-603, April 1962
         Concerning Hill v. United States, 368
         U.S. 424 (1962).

Glueck, Sheldon
The sentencing problem; before Judicial Conference of the
Third Circuit United States Courts, Atlantic City, September
12, 1956. Federal Probation 20: 15-25, December 1956
         Concerning individualization of sentence,
         disparities in sentencing and devices for
         achieving uniformity.

Goodman, Louis E.
In defense of federal judicial sentencing. California Law
Review 46: 497-507, October 1958

Hartshorne, Richard
The 1958 federal "split-sentence" law [Pub.L. 85-741]. Federal Probation 23: 9-12, June 1959

Hoffman, Walter E.
A sentencing philosophy; before Seminars for New Federal
Judges, held by Judicial Conference of the United States,
1968. Federal Probation 32: 3-8, December 1968
Same: revised December 30, 1969. 40p Washington, D.C.,
U.S. Administrative Office of the United States Courts,
1969.

International Penal and Penitentiary Foundation
Studies in penology dedicated to the memory of Sir Lionel
Fox; edited by Manuel Lopez-Rey and Charles Germain. 239p
The Hague, Martinus Nijoff, 1964
Ahead of his time, by James V. Bennett,
p. 42-49.
Concerning extensions of Federal
Youth Corrections Act and sentenc-
ing practices in federal courts.

Meth, Theodore S.
Sentencing the recidivist--an ethical dilemma. Kentucky Law
Journal 51: 711-19, Summer 1963
Concerning sentencing function of the
federal judiciary in cases of draft regis-
trants refusing to accept civilian work
in lieu of military training.

Rubin, Sol
Sentencing goals: real and ideal. Federal Probation 21: 51-
56, June 1957
Comment: Further comments on the sentencing problem, by Sheldon Glueck. Federal Probation 21: 47-54, December 1957.

Sharp, Louis J.
Modern sentencing in federal courts: the effect on probation
and parole. American University Law Review 12: 167-77, June
1963

Smith, George P., II
Title 28, Section 2255 of the United State Code--motion to
vacate, set aside, or correct sentence: effective or ineffec-
tive aid to a federal prisoner? Notre Dame Law Review 40:
171-90, February 1965

Smith, Talbot
　The sentencing council and the problem of disproportionate
　sentences; before Seminar on Sentencing Theories and Tech-
　niques, Queens University, Kingston, June 5, 1962.　Federal
　Probation 27: 5-9, June 1963
　　　　　　　Concerning Council of Eastern District of
　　　　　　　Michigan.
　Same: Professional responsibility: the sentencing council and
　the problem of disproportionate sentences.　Practical Lawyer
　(2): 12-21, February 1965.

Steele, Walter W., Jr.
　Counsel can count in federal sentencing.　American Bar Assoc-
　iation, Journal 56: 37-40, January 1970
　　　　　　　Concerning a federal probation officer's
　　　　　　　report in determination of a sentence.

A symposium on sentencing alternatives in the federal courts.
　Federal Probation 26: 3-56, June 1962
　　　　　　　Sentencing alternatives available to the
　　　　　　　courts, by William F. Smith;
　　　　　　　Observation and study of defendants prior
　　　　　　　to sentence, by Charles E. Smith;
　　　　　　　Sentencing the adult offender, by Eugene
　　　　　　　N. Barkin;
　　　　　　　Sentencing the youth and young adult of-
　　　　　　　fender, by A. E. Gottshall;
　　　　　　　Sentencing the juvenile offender, by John
　　　　　　　F. Byerly;
　　　　　　　Federal parole policies and practices, by
　　　　　　　Richard A. Chappell;
　　　　　　　Sentencing methods and techniques in the
　　　　　　　United States, by B.J. George, Jr.;
　　　　　　　If I were a judge, by Albert Wahl;
　　　　　　　The professional character of the presen-
　　　　　　　tence report, by Paul W. Keve.

U.S. Administrative Office of the United States Courts
　Federal offenders in the United States district courts,
　1964.　87p　(process)　Washington, D.C., 1965
　　　　　　　Includes for the first time a weighting
　　　　　　　scheme for indicating the severity of
　　　　　　　sentences imposed for different groups
　　　　　　　of offenders, districts, etc.

　Persons under the supervision of the federal probation sys-
　tem, 1968.　159p (process)　Washington, D.C., 1970
　　　　　　　Table: Defendants sentenced by type of
　　　　　　　sentence, by district, p. 146.

U.S. Bureau of Prisons
Desk book for sentencing. (preliminary draft) 116p (mim)
Washington, D.C., April 1961

Remedies available to an inmate to challenge sentence; by
Frederick W. Hearn. Its Progress Report 9: 11-15, July-
September 1961

Score card on 4208 (b) cases. Its Progress Report 9: 16-17,
July-September 1961
        Concerning Title 18, United States Code,
        sentencing law, operative August 25, 1958.

U.S. Congress. House. Committee on the District of Columbia.
Subcommittees No. 1 and 3
Anti-crime proposals; hearing [on H.R. 13689, H.R. 12854,
H.R. 13690, H.R. 12855, H.R. 12856, H.R. 8781, H.R. 6034],
September 22, October 1, 7, 14, November 4, 10, 17, 1969.
337, 136p (91:1) Washington, D.C., 1969
        Pt. 1 includes right of government to be
        heard at sentencing and stiffer mandatory
        sentences;
        Pt. 2 includes mandatory sentences for first
        and second offenses.

U.S. Congress. House. Committee on the Judiciary
Rules of Criminal Procedure for the United States District
Courts, as amended. 40p Washington, D.C., April 20, 1962
Same: 45p 1966
        C. 7: Sentence and judgment.

U.S. Congress. Senate
S. 2932, to provide for reducing sentences of imprisonment
imposed upon persons held in custody for want of bail of the
time so spent in custody; House amendments in nature of sub-
stitute, agreed to by Senate. Congressional Record, August
24, 1960: 17464

S. 1956, to clarify provisions of law authorizing the commitment of a defendant to the custody of the Attorney General for a study after conviction; statement. Congressional
Record, July 30, 1963: 13656-57

U.S. Congress. Senate. Committee on the District of Columbia
Statement on H.R. 7525, an act relating to crime and criminal procedure in the District of Columbia; by James V. Bennett. 14p (mim) Washington, D.C., November 6, 1963
        Concerning penalty provisions for burglary
        and robbery.
Comment: Federal Probation 27: 77, December 1963.

U.S. Congress. Senate. Committee on the Judiciary
  The federal prison system--1964; hearing before Subcommittee
  on National Penitentiaries, January 22, 1964. 481p (88:2)
  Washington, D.C., 1964
            Appendix:
            Sentencing: the judge's problem, by Irv-
            ing R. Kaufman;
            Symposium on sentencing alternatives in
            the federal courts, by William F. Smith
            and others;
            Seminar and Institute on Disparity of
            Sentences for Sixth, Seventh and Eighth
            Judicial Circuits;
            Highland Park Institute on Sentence Dis-
            parity, by Frank Remington and Donald J.
            Newman;
            Appellate review of sentences; a sympos-
            ium at the Judicial Conference of the
            U.S. Court of Appeals for the Second Cir-
            cuit, Manchester, Vt., September 24, 1962.

  Organized crime control act of 1969; report to accompany
  S. 20. 218p (91:1, S.Rep. no. 617) Washington, D.C.,
  December 18, 1969
            Title 10: Dangerous special offender sen-
            tencing.

U.S. Court of Appeals, Tenth Circuit
  Proceedings at the 1969 Judicial Conference, July 1-3, 1969;
  edited by William L. Whittaker. Federal Rules Decisions
  49-50: 347-612, 1970
            Includes: Pleas of guilty, sentencing alter-
            natives and procedures.

U.S. District Court, Northern District of Illinois
  [Sentencing council.] Federal Probation 28: 67, March 1964

U.S. District Court, Eastern District of Michigan
  The Federal Sentencing Council: an attempt at disparity re-
  duction; by Lynn D. Sigurdson. Thesis (M._), University of
  Michigan, School of Social Work, 1964
  Abstract:· International Bibliography on Crime and Delin-
  quency 3: 57, August 1965.

  [First Sentencing Council established at Detroit in 1960.]
  Federal Probation 28: 67, March 1964

  [Sentencing Council; first full year of operation, fiscal
  1962.] NCCD News (National Council on Crime and Delinquency)
  44: 10, September-October 1965

U.S. Judicial Conference of the United States
  Desk book for sentencing; prepared by Committee on the Admin-
  istration of Criminal Law for first Seminar and Institute on
  Sentencing, Boulder, July 1959. v.p. (process) Washington,
  D.C., June 1962
          Concerning presentence procedure, proba-
          tion, commitment authority, parole, fed-
          eral prison system, and mental incompetency.

  Preliminary draft of proposed amendments to Rules of Criminal Procedure for the United States District Courts; prepared by Committee on Rules of Practice and Procedure.
  Federal Rules Decisions 48: 547-647, 1970
          Includes: Sentence and judgment, and pre-
          sentence investigation.

  Report of the proceedings...March 13-14, and September 20-
  21, 1961.... 342p Washington, D.C., 1962
          Includes: Report of Committee on the Ad-
          ministration of the Criminal Law (appel-
          late review of sentences and mandatory
          minimum sentences).

  Report of the proceedings...March 8-9, September 19-20, 1962
  .... 296p Washington, D.C., 1962
          Includes: Report of Committee on the Ad-
          ministration of the Criminal Law (appel-
          late review of sentences, indeterminate
          sentences, institutes on sentencing).

  Report of the proceedings...March 16-17, and September 23-
  24, 1964.... 304p Washington, D.C., 1964
          Includes: Report of Committee on the Ad-
          ministration of the Criminal Law (appel-
          late review of sentences).

  Report of the proceedings...March 13-14, 1969, June 10, 1969
  and October 31-November 1, 1969.... 387p Washington, D.C.,
  1970
          Includes: Report of Committee on the Ad-
          ministration of the Criminal Law (appel-
          late review of sentencing).

Youth Corrections Act sentencing provisions. Federal Probation 21: 57-58, June 1957
          Federal Youth Corrections Act in opera-
          tion since January 1954 in all judicial
          circuits except the Eighth, Ninth, Tenth
          and Texas and Louisiana in the Fifth.

District of Columbia

Medalie, Richard J.
 The offender rehabilitation project: a new role for defense
 counsel at pretrial and sentencing. Georgetown Law Journal
 56: 2-16, November 1967
            Concerning District of Columbia Legal Aid
            Agency rehabilitation project in criminal
            courts.

U.S. Department of Justice. Office of Criminal Justice
 Criminal justice in a metropolitan court; the processing of
 serious criminal cases in the District of Columbia Court of
 General Sessions; by Harry I. Subin. 209p Washington, D.C.,
 October 1966
            Sentencing, p. 88-90.

U.S. President's Commission on Crime in the District of Columbia
 Report. 1041, 777p Washington, D.C., December 15, 1966
            Sentencing, imprisonment and supervision
            of the adult offender, p. 368-473.

STANDARDS FOR SENTENCING

"In undertaking to prepare a Model Sentencing Act, the Advisory Council of Judges determined to move the penal law onto a new and higher level. Instead of 'rectification' of the existing pattern of codes," the Council's "goal was a statute conforming to the best concepts of modern penology. The Act is a welding of two intimately related developments...probation, based on a proper presentence investigation... [and] the recognition that prolonged incarceration is necessary for certain individuals whose behavior patterns and personality make them highly dangerous to society."

> National Council on Crime and Delinquency. Advisory Council of Judges
> Model Sentencing Act. 35p New York, 1963
> Same: Crime and Delinquency 9: 339-69, October 1963.

Materials relating to the Model Sentencing Act include the following--

Edwards, George
Sentencing the racketeer. Crime and Delinquency 9: 391-97, October 1963

Flood, Gerald F.
The Model Sentencing Act; a higher level of penal law. Crime and Delinquency 9: 370-80, October 1963

Guides to the judge in sentencing in racketeering cases. Crime and Delinquency 14: 97-106, April 1968

Guttmacher, Manfred S.
Dangerous offenders. Crime and Delinquency 9: 381-90, October 1963

Murrah, Alfred P. and Rubin, Sol
Penal reform and the Model Sentencing Act. Columbia Law Review 65: 1167-79, November 1965

National Conference on the Churches and Social Welfare
[Model Sentencing Act; by Milton G. Rector, before meeting, Cleveland, October 25, 1961.] NCCD News (National Council on Crime and Delinquency) 40: 4, November 1961

Powers, Sanger B.
A correctional administrator's view of the Model Sentencing Act. Crime and Delinquency 9: 398-403, October 1963

Rector, Milton G.
  Sentencing the racketeer.   Crime and Delinquency 8: 385-89,
  October 1962

Rubin, Sol
  The Model Sentencing Act; before fourth annual Institute of
  Judges, Indiana Citizens Council on Crime and Delinquency,
  August 23, 1963. New York University Law Review 39: 251-62,
  April 1964

Materials relating to other standards for sentencing include
the following--

Council of State Governments. Committee of State Officials on
  Suggested State Legislation
  Suggested state legislation, 1965. v.24 212p Chicago, Oc-
  tober 1964
          Includes: Model Penal Code, Model Senten-
          cing Act.

Doub, George C.
  Recent trends in the criminal law. American Bar Association,
  Journal 46: 139-42, February 1960
          Concerning problem of setting standards
          to guide judges in imposing sentences.

National Council on Crime and Delinquency
  Model sentencing act for misdemeanors; by Sol Rubin [to be
  presented to Council of Judges, May 1971]. New York, 1971

National Council on Crime and Delinquency. Council of Judges
  Guides to sentencing the dangerous offender. 21p New
  York, 1969
          To assist in application of Model Senten-
          cing Act.

National Council on Crime and Delinquency and Institute for
  the Study and Treatment of Delinquency
  Crime and delinquency; a rational approach to penal problems; by Sol Rubin. ed.2 248p New York, Oceana Publications, 1961
          Concerning Standard Juvenile Court Act.

National Probation and Parole Association. National Advisory
  Council of Judges
  Guides for sentencing. 99p New York, 1957
          Appendix B: Presentence investigation re-
          ports.

American Bar Association

American Bar Association. Project on Minimum Standards for
Criminal Justice
Standards relating to appellate review of sentences (tenta-
tive draft); recommended by the Advisory Committee on Sen-
tencing and Review. 160p New York, Institute of Judicial
Administration, April 1967
        Appendix A: Review statutes;
        Appendix B: Federal and state proposals;
        Appendix C: The review of criminal senten-
        ces in England, by Daniel J. Meador;
        Appendix D: Selected bibliography.

Standards relating to criminal appeals (tentative draft);
recommended by the Advisory Committee on Sentencing and Review. 109p New York, Institute of Judicial Administration,
March 1969
        Selected bibliography, p. 101-109.

Standards relating to pleas of guilty (tentative draft); recommended by the Advisory Committee on the Criminal Trial.
78p New York, Institute of Judicial Administration, February
1967
____; Amendments recommended by the Special Committee on
Minimum Standards for the Administration of Criminal Justice
and concurred in by a majority of the Advisory Committee....
5p March 1968
        Concerning plea discussions, plea agree-
        ments and withdrawal of the plea.

Standards relating to post-conviction remedies (tentative
draft); recommended by the Advisory Committee on Sentencing
and Review. 123p New York, Institute of Judicial Administration, January 1967
        Appendix C: Table of post-conviction acts;
        Appendix D: Selected bibliography.

Standards relating to probation (tentative draft); recommended by the Advisory Committee on Sentencing and Review.
110p New York, Institute of Judicial Administration, February 1970
        Appendix: Selected bibliography.

Standards relating to sentencing alternatives and procedures
(tentative draft); recommended by the Advisory Committee on
Sentencing and Review. 345p New York, Institute of Judicial Administration, December 1967
        Appendix B: Model Penal Code sentencing
        provisions;
        Appendix C: Model Sentencing Act.

American Law Institute

American Law Institute
  Model Penal Code; tentative draft no. 9, 1959. 220, 84p
  Philadelphia, May 8, 1959
          Appendix D: Statutory provisions governing
          discretion with respect to sentence of
          death;
          Appendix E: Prison sentences for murder
          and eligibility for parole in non-capital
          punishment states;
          Appendix F: Eligibility for parole of pri-
          soners serving life imprisonment for murder
          in capital punishment jurisdictions.

  Model Penal Code; proposed official draft, May 4, 1962.
  346p Philadelphia, 1962
          Authority of court in sentencing, p. 106-22.

Goodrich, Herbert F.
  To make the punishment fit the crime. Shingle (Philadelphia
  Bar Association) 20: 193-95, November 1957

Grad, Frank P.
  The A.L.I. Model Penal Code. NPPA Journal (National Probation and Parole Association) 4: 127-38, April 1958

Moreland, Roy
  Model Penal Code: sentencing, probation and parole. Kentucky Law Journal 57: 51-82, Fall 1968-69

Rubin, Sol
  Sentencing and correctional treatment under the Law Institute's Model Penal Code. American Bar Association, Journal
  46: 994-98, September 1960
  Comment: Sentencing, correction, and the Model Penal Code,
  by Herbert Wechsler. University of Pennsylvania Law Review 109: 465-93, February 1961.

Schwartz, Louis B.
  The Model Penal Code: an invitation to law reform. American
  Bar Association, Journal 49: 447-55, May 1963

Wechsler, Herbert
  Sentencing and correction under the Model Penal Code. Amer-
  ican Correctional Association, Annual Congress of Correction,
  Proceedings 90: 65-70, 1960

SENTENCING IN VARIOUS COUNTRIES

"In a great many countries legislative attention has been given to the sentencing process itself and to appellate review of sentences." The United States is "the only country in the free world where a single judge may, without being subjected to any review of his determination on the merits, decide absolutely the minimum period of time during which a convicted offender must remain in prison."

> George, B. J., Jr.
> An unsolved problem; comparative sentencing techniques [in other countries]. American Bar Association, Journal 45: 250-54, March 1959

Materials relating to sentencing in various countries include the following--

Abe, Haruo and George, B. J., Jr.
Sentencing and treatment, the growing emphasis on therapeutic and preventive aspects of criminal justice in Japan; prepared for final Conference of the Japanese-American Program for Cooperation in Legal Studies, Cambridge, September 5-9, 1961. 82p (mim) July 30, 1961

Barry, John Vincent William
The courts and criminal punishments. 91p Wellington, N.Z., Government Printer, 1969
> Concerning the sentencing function of the courts.

Canada. Minister of Justice
Report of Committee Appointed to Inquire Into the Principles and Procedures Followed in the Remission Service of the Department of Justice. Ottawa, 1956
Summary: Summary of recommendations of [Gerald] Fauteux report. American Journal of Correction 21: 29-31, January-February 1959.

Canadian Congress of Corrections
Papers, third biennial Congress, Toronto, May 14-19, 1961.
Canadian Journal of Corrections 3: 205-404, April 1961
> Sentencing, by J. C. McRuer;
> Individualization of sentence, by M. S. Guttmacher;
> Problems of sentencing, by T. George Street.

Canadian Corrections Association
    Proposals for development of probation in Canada.   35p   (mim)
    Ottawa, February 1, 1967
            Concerning presentence reports as privi-
            leged communications.

Cheffins, R. I. and Others
    Some psychological aspects of sentencing; before symposium
    on sentencing, Second Annual Research Conference on Crimi-
    nology and Delinquency, Montreal, May 1960.   Canadian Journal
    of Corrections 3: 66-86, January 1961

Cormier, Bruno M. and Others
    The persistent offender; summary of a seminar held on June 5,
    1963 at the Canadian Congress of Corrections.   Canadian Jour-
    nal of Corrections 5: 253-61, October 1963
            Includes: Sentencing.

Council of Europe. European Committee on Crime
    Suspended-sentence, probation and other alternatives to pri-
    son sentences.   128p   Strasbourg, 1966

Dalhousie Law School
    Judicial conference on sentencing March 3, 1962.   Journal of
    Criminal Law... 53: 232-33, June 1962

Discrepancies in sentencing in magistrates' courts: is there
    a remedy?   Criminal Law Review 1963: 253-61, April 1963

Drapkin S., Israel
    Criminological aspects of sentencing.   In his Studies in
    Criminology, p. 28-52.   Jerusalem, Hebrew University, 1969
    Abstract: Crime and Delinquency Literature 2: 394-95,
    August 1970

Edwards, J. Ll. J.
    Sentencing, corrections and the prevention of crime; before
    the ninth Alumni Conference on Crime and Punishment, Uni-
    versity of Manitoba, March 19, 1966.   Canadian Journal of
    Corrections 8: 186-201, July 1966

Fox, Sir Lionel W.
    The sentence and rehabilitation; before Criminal Law Sec-
    tion, American Bar Association, July 29, 1957.   Federal Pro-
    bation 22: 15-18, March 1968

Great Britain. Home Office
    The sentence of the court: a handbook for courts on the treat-
    ment of offenders.   ed.2   75p   London, H.M.Stationery Office,
    1969

Great Britain. Home Office. Interdepartmental Committee on the
  Business of the Criminal Courts
  Report. 143p (Cmd. 1289) London, H.M.Stationery Office,
  February 1961
          C. 9: Sentencing.
  Comment: Theories of punishment in the Court of Appeal, by
  D. A. Thomas. Modern Law Review 27: 546-67, September 1964.

Halmos, Paul, ed.
  Sociological studies in the British penal services. Socio-
  logical Review Monograph (University of Keele) (9): 5-252,
  June 1965
          Sentencing policy, by W. J. H. Sprott;
          Sentencing by magistrates: some facts of
          life, by R. F. Sparks.

Hays, Glenn
  Towards uniformity of sentence. Canadian Journal of Corrections 9: 115-21, April 1967

Hogarth, John
  Towards the improvement of sentencing in Canada. Canadian
  Journal of Corrections 9: 122-36, April 1967

Hood, Roger
  Sentencing in magistrates' courts; a study in variation of
  policy. 145p London, Stevens, 1962
          Bibliography, p. 141-42.

  A study of the effectiveness of presentence investigations
  in reducing recidivism. British Journal of Criminology 6:
  303-10, July 1966
          "Presentence reports have not reduced
          reconviction rates."

Hopkins, B. W.
  The problem of sentencing; before Regional Conference of
  After-care Agencies and Government Services, Hamilton, Feb-
  ruary 17, 1958. Canadian Bar Journal 1: 33-48, October 1958

Hughes, S. H. S.
  Some comments on sentencing; before Conference of Magistrates
  of Ontario, October 4, 1964. Canadian Bar Journal 8: 221-
  29+, August 1965

Jaffary, Stuart K.
  Sentencing of adults in Canada. 122p (Studies in the criminal sciences no. 1) Toronto, University of Toronto Press,
  1963

John Howard Society of Alberta
    Sentencing: some social and legal issues; by J. W. Anderson
    before sixth annual Red Deer Conference, October 20, 1962.
    9p Calgary, Ca., [1962]

Kirkpatrick, A. M.
    Confidentiality in the correctional services. Canadian Jour-
    nal of Corrections 5: 114-28, April 1963

McFarlane, G. G.
    Theory and development of presentence reports in Ontario.
    Canadian Journal of Corrections 7: 201-24, April 1965
            Includes: Summary of 1962 British Depart-
            mental Committee proposals compared with
            Ontario policy and practices in 1963; Use
            of presentence reports in U.S.A.

Meeker, Ben S.
    Probation as a sentence; before Recent Developments in Crim-
    inology and Corrections Lectures, Centre of Criminology,
    University of Toronto, February 1966. Canadian Journal of
    Corrections 9: 281-305, October 1967

Queen's University. Law School
    Proceedings of the seminar on the sentencing of offenders
    [June 4-15, 1962]; edited by Alan W. Mewett. 47p Kingston,
    Ontario, 1962
    Excerpt: The sentencing council and the problem of dispro-
    portionate sentences, by Talbot Smith. Federal Probation
    27: 5-9, June 1963.

Raeburn, Walter
    The bespoke sentence. British Journal of Criminology 5:
    266-74, July 1965

Samuels, Alec
    Extended sentences. New Law Journal 120: 146-47, February
    12, 1970

Scott, G. W.
    Sentencing; before Western Regional Conference on Parole and
    After Care, February 1958. Canadian Journal of Corrections
    1: 6-14, April 1959

Shoham, Shlomo
    Sentencing policy of criminal courts in Israel. Journal of
    Criminal Law... 50: 327-37, November-December 1959
            Excerpt from Thesis, Hebrew University,
            Jerusalem.

Street, T. G. and Others
    Could inequality of sentences be reduced if sentencing were
    left to a sentencing board.... Canadian Journal of Correc-
    tions 5: 48-57, January 1963

Toronto, Ont. University. Centre of Criminology
    Proceedings of the National Conference of Judges on Sentenc-
    ing, May 27-29, 1964. 70p Toronto, September 1964
            The responsibilities of the sentencing
            judge and the necessity for adequate in-
            formation in selecting the appropriate form
            of sentence, by Dana Porter;
            The factors and considerations affecting the
            carrying out of a judge's sentencing respon-
            sibilities, by Lucien Tremblay;
            Recent developments in the federal peniten-
            tiaries and their relevance to the judge's
            sentencing responsibilities, by A. J. McLeod.

White, Stephen
    Suspended sentences--recent developments. New Law Journal
    120: 17-18, 41-43, January 1-8, 1970

Williams, J. E. Hall
    The sentencing policy of the Court of Criminal Appeal. How-
    ard Journal (Howard League for Penal Reform) 10 (3): 201-11,
    1960

LIST OF CASES

INDEX

91

Publications

of the

INSTITUTE OF GOVERNMENTAL STUDIES

University of California

Berkeley

Juvenile Gangs and Street Groups—a Bibliography; Compiled
by Dorothy C. Tompkins. 88p   1966 $1.75

White Collar Crime—a Bibliography; Compiled by Dorothy C.
Tompkins. 85p   1967 $3.00

The Confession Issue—From McNabb to Miranda, a Bibliography; Compiled by Dorothy C. Tompkins. 100p   1968 $3.00

Poverty in the United States During the Sixties—a Bibliography; Compiled by Dorothy C. Tompkins. 542p   1970
                                              $10.00 paperbound
                                              $13.50 clothbound

[California residents add 5% sales tax]